HOW TO *Really* TALK ABOUT BOOKS YOU HAVEN'T READ

Also by Henry Hitchings

Dr Johnson's Dictionary
The Secret Life of Words

HOW TO *Really* TALK ABOUT BOOKS YOU HAVEN'T READ

HENRY HITCHINGS

JOHN MURRAY

First published in Great Britain in 2008 by John Murray (Publishers)
An Hachette Livre UK company

1

A CIP catalogue record for this title is available from the British Library

ISBN 978-1-84854-009-5

Typeset in Monotype Bembo by Servis Filmsetting Ltd, Stockport, Cheshire

Printed and bound by Clays Ltd, St Ives plc

John Murray policy is to use papers that are natural, renewable and recyclable products
and made from wood grown in sustainable forests. The logging and manufacturing
processes are expected to conform to the environmental regulations of the country
of origin.

John Murray (Publishers)
338 Euston Road
London NW1 3BH

www.johnmurray.co.uk

CONTENTS

1

FIRST THINGS FIRST: *WHY* TO TALK ABOUT BOOKS YOU HAVEN'T READ?

You are at a wedding or a dinner party, and the conversation is flowing – a roiling, competitive brabble. Or perhaps it is edgy, hesitant (though still competitive). But then the subject moves on . . . to books. The change in direction is an opportunity for you to look either brilliant or ridiculous, and you sense this keenly. Which will it be?

A few years ago I came across a party game that reveals the anxieties involved in this question. The game requires each player to think of a book with which everyone else will be familiar but which he or she has not read. To illustrate: if while guzzling my goldfish bowl of Pinot Grigio I claim ignorance of *Gulliver's Travels* and everyone else present has read it, I achieve full marks. (The liars, though! They've only read the first two sections, about the little folk of Lilliput and the big people of Brobdingnag, without getting on to the heavy stuff about noble horses, deformed degenerate humans, and cranky scientists trying to extract sunbeams from cucumbers.) But if I nominate, say, Halldor Laxness's *Independent People*, an Icelandic novel apparently much concerned with sheep, their turds and the weather, and if no one else has read it either, I fare badly.

The problem here is pretty obvious. In order to win, I need to make an embarrassing confession – revealing my unfamiliarity with something I would probably be expected to know. On the other hand, if I'm too proud to divulge the name of a book unknown to me that others are likely to have read, I lose. This calls for a kind of social game theory: what price am I prepared to pay for victory? In the novel *Changing Places* by David Lodge, the writer who has been credited with inventing the game, it is played by literature scholars, and is won by a dislikeable American, Howard Ringbaum, who to general amazement announces that he has never read *Hamlet*. In order to win he has to go so far as to ruin his professional credibility.

The game, which Lodge fittingly calls 'Humiliation', highlights the degree to which not knowing about certain iconic books is regarded as a blunder. In the context of Humiliation, this blunder has its reward. But in just about any other situation, it does not. Usually we are rewarded for what we do know, rather than what we are willing to admit we don't, and one of the reasons you might talk about a book you haven't read is to avoid appearing philistine or uninformed. You don't want to be the person who thinks that George Eliot was a man and wrote the lyrics for *Cats*. You don't want to sound clueless when everyone else is enthusing about the big-screen version of Ian McEwan's *Atonement*. Alternatively, you might do it in order to maintain the image of expertise that Howard Ringbaum woefully loses: an art historian probably ought to have read a ground-breaking new work on Caravaggio, and a nightclub doorman should have digested the latest page-turner about bare-knuckle boxing in the Black Country.

There are plenty of other reasons, though. Maybe you do it because you want to keep up the flow of talk with someone you find interesting; it's a form of flirting or flattery. Or you do it because you are a risk-taker – you wouldn't know Flaubert if he stood up in your soup. Maybe, too, you think that humans are fundamentally deceitful, and you don't want to fight that tendency. You might also do it to discover if you ought to read this particular book, or need to – in a spirit of curiosity rather than duplicity. And you could also be attempting one-upmanship, that sport of obtrusive and hollow superiority.

You might do it to avoid talking about something less palatable; for talking about books, whether you have read them or not, seems more like fun than talking about mortgages or babies. You talk about a book you have not read because you know the person to whom you are talking hasn't read it either. 'This could be amusing,' you think, 'I could really get away with this.' Perhaps you want to do justice to an impression of yourself that you have artfully created: as polymath and intellectual sharpshooter. Or you do it in error; because you think you have read the book, because it sounds like something you might have read, because you dimly recall dipping into it, or because your memories are confused and you are influenced by having seen it for sale, reviewed or advertised.

But let's now turn the question on its head. Why wouldn't you talk about a book you haven't read? For fear of exposure as a fraud. Out of intellectual integrity. Because you know you are a bad liar. Because you are not a liar at all. Or because it threatens to return you to a familiar nightmare, in which you arrive to sit an exam for which you are meant to be peachily prepared, only to find when you put pen to paper that all your knowledge and all your skills and all your confidence have deserted you.

As you can see, this list of reasons is shorter than the previous one. The reasons contained in it are substantial, but if you are genuinely troubled by them you are unlikely to succeed in talking about books you haven't read, because the art of doing so involves a good deal of effrontery.

This art feels necessary because, it seems, there are certain books which any civilized person ought to have read. If you winced at that last sentence, thank you: there are several things about it that are objectionable, not least of them the vile 'any civilized person'. Nevertheless, there's a nagging awareness that educated people are expected to have a hands-on knowledge of authors such as Tolstoy and Dostoevsky, and of works such as *The Divine Comedy* and *Ulysses*. Step into a bookshop, even a poorly stocked one, and you'll be overcome by the sense that the volumes on its shelves contain a wealth of things you ought to know or to have seen. There is just so much to comprehend. You can read two new books a week and consider yourself impressively up to speed, but you are still reading only a tiny fraction of 1 per cent of the titles actually being published. Many of those titles are all but unreadable – specialist works on, say, computer operating systems or professional horticulture – yet a vast amount of eminently readable and informative or inspiring writing escapes us every week, and we're never going to be able to catch up with it. In even trying to, we quickly end up print-drunk.

This is something felt by all readers, whether keen or occasional, and it results in a good deal of anxiety and deception.

After all, so many other people seem ever ready with some nugget of philosophy or a poetic gem. The effect can be humbling. P. G. Wodehouse's immortal butler Jeeves often quotes Shakespeare, whom Wodehouse himself rather jauntily referred to as 'my brother author'. On one occasion, Jeeves's master Bertie Wooster is describing his opponent in an upcoming darts competition. Recalling a line of Lady Macbeth's, he says that this person, when reminded of their imminent match, stands 'goggling like a cat in an adage'. The adage in question, learnt from Jeeves, is about the hazards of 'letting "I dare not" wait upon "I would"'; it relates to a cat that wants to eat fish, but is not prepared to get its feet wet to do so. Bertie is haunted by this image, which is relevant here not only because it is an example of the way Shakespeare crops up in the most unlikely places (Bertie Wooster? A darts competition?), but also because, when we talk about a book we haven't read, the paltry fears of 'I dare not' must not be allowed to encroach on our resolve. You can't be defensive: you have to be creative.

Why don't people read?

A different question now – and specifically, why don't more people read more for pleasure? Among the explanations that get lobbed around are that it is difficult, requires more concentration than other leisure activities, and is expensive. In Martin Amis's novel *Money* (1984) the main character, John Self, inspects the habitat of his creator: 'I tell you, this Martin Amis, he lives like a student . . . Why isn't he living right up to the hilt of his dough? He must have a bad book-habit.' The money spent on rare editions and glistening hardbacks could surely, he thinks, be more productively invested.

All this learning and dust-gathering cleverness tends to be seen as nerdy or pretentious. The adjective 'bookish' has been used scathingly for 400 years; in the second part of Shakespeare's *Henry VI*, the Duke of York declares that Henry's 'bookish rule' has 'pulled fair England down'. Bookishness is the opposite of the ability to get stuff done. Try searching the internet for the words 'bookish dictator' – the last time I did so I got just one hit, and it was from a Canadian blog about comics.

In addition, people complain of not having enough time for books. They say they have overdosed on reading at work or in school – those drab annual reports, those mildewed poems about autumn and funerals. Maybe, too, they lack a quiet and peaceful place in which to read. True, there's the loo, but that's only good for *Heat* magazine – or this book. They may also complain of being slow or incompetent readers, like the child who confesses, 'Teacher, I was too busy reading the book to understand it.' The behaviour of reading may not have been ingrained early enough. Books are too long. Their subject matter does not have much to do with day-to-day life: how often do you find yourself employed as Commissar of Cat Control, or coming upon a severed nose in your freshly baked morning loaf, or transformed overnight into a monstrous, verminous bug? Plus, modern printed volumes are cumbersome – according to one friend, 'If a book's bigger than a DVD, I'm going to bed with the DVD.' Or, as a former colleague imparted, 'Only a man would want to surround himself with all that dead . . . like, *wood*.' In any case, the reader has to do all the work. There are far too many hard words. Following those serpentine sentences is soporific. It's enough, the mindless objector shrieks, to give a person eyestrain. It'll make you feel stupid. It's a hassle. The rest of the world doesn't really care about what you have read. By the time a book is published, it is already . . . what's the word? *Obsolete.*

Unquestionably, there are some seductive alternatives to reading. Anyone who has ever tried to be an advocate for books will have heard all about the magnetic appeal of the latest computer game, cult TV series, website or band. Other media seem more urgent, their landscapes more impressive. Evidently, there are more distractions now than confronted, say, Dickens or Wordsworth or Proust. Shakespeare may have been at risk of getting stabbed in the eye, like his fellow dramatist Christopher Marlowe, but he wasn't infernally busy editing his iTunes playlists or updating his MySpace profile. Reading may easily be neglected or forgotten when we are absorbed in matters to do with our health, our responsibilities to family and friends, or our jobs and homes and finances. Most of us have become preoccupied with such concerns. A further claim is that the spread of literacy has allowed us to take reading for granted, with complacency becoming the norm: illiteracy has given way to *alliteracy*.

Of course, some kinds of reading are in rude health. We devour the text of emails, confidential business documents and the free newspapers we find discarded on the train. We fuss over instruction manuals and information about things we consume – the ingredients on the packaging for a ready meal, say, or the superfluous blather on the back of a bottle of wine. Every day we pay close attention to advertisements and signs. But literature is a different matter. 'Books are a load of crap,' wrote

Philip Larkin. An ironic thing for a poet to say, and especially for a poet who worked as a librarian. But then, like so much of Larkin's writing, the judgement seems a challenge to itself. In this case it is also a parody of the kind of philistine mockery to which poets and librarians have to grow accustomed.

One of the problems with the opposite argument – that books are nourishing and vital – is that it sounds mawkish. Literature can help us make sense of the everyday, can locate us in the world (can help us locate our souls, I might even risk claiming), and can enable us to see more keenly the structure of our feelings and perceptions. When we recognize the experiences of a character in a novel, the recognition contributes to our understanding of our selves. More than that, the book becomes a part of this understanding. The literary works that add most to our self-awareness and self-knowledge are part of our personal history, as important as 'real' experiences. We remember them intensely.

To say these things is by no means easy; they seem to suggest not only earnestness, a cloying sincerity, but also self-involvement, a disconnection from normality – from the real world of bills, hangovers and bathroom aromas. Reading is one of the pleasures of solitude, and its rewards are (mostly) selfish. They are also hard to convey to those who have not tasted them. As much as anything, you cannot teach a person the art of being alone.

It is an assumption of this book that you do read – what are you doing now, after all? – but this assumption runs in parallel with a suspicion: that you find yourself in situations where you want or need to dissemble, to pretend to know more than you really do.

Two views of reading

A. 'Reading makes immigrants of us all. It takes us away from home, but, more important, it finds homes for us everywhere.' (Jean Rhys, author of *Wide Sargasso Sea*)
B. ' "Tell me what you read and I'll tell you who you are" is true enough, but I'd know you better if you told me what you reread.' (François Mauriac, 1952 Nobel laureate)

Through the pages that follow, even as books are championed, there will run a vein of suspicion: sometimes, surely, we are too reverent about books, and we are too reverent about reading. The sixteenth-century essayist Michel de Montaigne took this view. Without a whiff of regret, he revealed that 'When I meet with difficulties in my reading, I do not bite my nails over them; after making one or two attempts I give them up.' 'If one book bores me,' he explained, 'I take up another; and I turn to reading only at such times as I begin to be tired of doing nothing.' Montaigne encourages us not to think books are sacred.

Our avid desire for knowledge – about how to get our new answerphone up and running, or about what happens to Rupert Campbell-Black at the end of the Rutshire Chronicles – causes us to skip or skim. Years ago a friend unblushingly told me that she tended to miss out the passages of description in novels and just read the dialogue – 'That's where the interesting stuff happens.' How I laughed. And yet, and yet . . . we have all at some time passed rapidly over an explanation, a passage of analysis, an indigestible-looking chunk of detail. Some readers, the opposites of my friend, skate over the dialogue; for them, the meat of the story is to be found elsewhere. Others ignore any paragraph that begins unpromisingly – for instance, 'The next day commenced as before' in Charlotte Brontë's *Jane Eyre*. But here's the thing: in different ways, and to differing degrees, everybody skates. Is there anyone who has read every word of *Bleak House* or *War and Peace*? Some people – such as a translator – will indignantly insist that the answer is 'Yes', but most of us read casually, and there is a real stigma attached to admitting this. People tend to be dishonest about their reading habits.

When I confess in public to not having finished a book, or to having skimmed it, I am greeted with looks of horror. I do actually tend to finish books, but I refuse to be detained by something that's not rewarding me. I say 'rewarding' rather than 'entertaining' because I am unlikely to be entertained by a grim novel about the withering of Western civilization, but I may be riveted and exercised by it. Telling a serious reader that you failed to finish a book, however, is a bit like telling your lover you are 'vaguely committed' to your relationship. An unfinished book is an accusation, staring at you menacingly.

Samuel Johnson, the endlessly quotable eighteenth-century man of letters, was adamant that books need not be consumed in their entirety. To his friend Hester Thrale he exclaimed, 'How few books are there of which one can ever possibly arrive at the *last* page!' This was shocking to his contemporaries. So was his response to a man who asked if he had read a new work that had attracted a good deal of admiration. 'I have looked into it,' Dr Johnson said. Pressed over whether he had 'read it through', he tartly replied, 'No, Sir; do *you* read books *through*?' Johnson's candour strikes us as unusual. His belief that one could begin a book in the middle or plunge into a volume in a 'fortuitous and unguided' fashion struck others as bordering on sacrilege. But Johnson's was in some surprising ways a modern sensibility, and he was astute in his understanding of the different types of reading it is possible to practise. He was also ahead of the game in recognizing that at the very same time that reading declines, the number of writers increases: 'writers will, perhaps, be multiplied, till no readers will be found.'

We're all writers these days, aren't we?

There is an old saying that to lead a full life one must raise a child, plant a tree and write a book. Now, an incomplete attempt at each is deemed enough. Everyone we meet seems to have a website, keep up a blog, script little snippets to broadcast on YouTube, scrawl *pensées* in a William-Morris-pattern journal, paint so-called clean graffiti, or send one of those artfully artless Christmas round-robin letters full of lines like 'Matilda aced her GCSEs and achieved a richly deserved merit in Grade 7 Oboe' or 'This year we discovered the hidden jewel that is Aix-en-Provence.' Dignified by type – Times New Roman, Arial or Garamond, according to taste – a person's words appear immortal. No author considers his or her output to be anything less than essential: 'My novel about a bizarre love triangle involving three twenty-something Oxbridge types? It just *has* to be written.' But then again, let's be honest: is there anywhere better furnished with evidence of the vanity of mankind's desires and ambitions than a library, where row upon row of books lie mouldering, untouched?

Nonetheless, to people who read, books have the ability both to heighten the senses and to anaesthetize them, to involve the mind yet also to beguile it. We hear of reading as escapism, but the word demeans the experience. (If reading is escapism, it is an escape *into* life, not away from it.) Reading is capable of absorbing people completely. At its most sublime, the concentration it requires feels effortless, and comprehension seems automatic. It can resemble eating and drinking; we sample books, and, as we engage with them more fully, gain an impression of their bouquet, their subtler flavours, their aftertaste. Some readers are gluttons, others nibblers. Dr Johnson was alleged to tear the heart out of a book 'like a Turk', and once surrendered a volume of Greek speeches because it was 'too fine for a scholar's talons'. Reading can be aggressive or delicate, just as it can be soothing or exhilarating. Sigmund Freud diagnosed the 'mild narcosis induced by art'; the experience is like dreaming while awake, and most readers know this opiate pleasure. Physiologically, reading is complex, and it causes arousal. That arousal can be erotic, visceral, intellectual, or of some other kind. Reading is a many-sided pleasure, as well as a precarious one. And it leads to conversations, with others and with ourselves.

Talking about books is a social activity: a pleasure of the table or of party-going; to be indulged over foaming pint glasses or a nursed dram of whiskey; the stuff of good-natured late-night rambles or fierce, invigorating confrontations; and perhaps even of the tennis court or the bedroom. *De gustibus non est disputandum*, insists the Latin proverb – in common parlance, there's no arguing about taste. This is plainly untrue. Taste is one of the things we argue about most often, and it is one of the things we are most inclined to argue about. I shall struggle to persuade a person whose favourite kind of ice cream is vanilla that prune and Armagnac flavour is actually better, but I can enjoy trying.

Personally, I hate arguing. But I must quote an old friend's riposte – 'So why the hell do you do it all the time?' One of the attractions of arguing is that it can transform what you know, think and understand. Argument is typically described in terms of conflict, yet it is also a mode of inquiry. As the Scottish philosopher David Hume observed, with a nod to Plato, 'Truth springs from argument amongst friends.' Ideas and values need to be tested, and argument achieves this. It is also a form of callisthenics for the mind. An intimate knowledge of the things we are disputing – Latin American politics, climate change, the relative merits of *Gossip Girl* and *Hollyoaks* – is less important than the value we derive from stretching our intellectual sinews. Culture *is* conversation.

Talking about books, whether you have read them or not, is deliciously conducive to argument. This argument can be exciting and productive. However, there are times when you should most definitely avoid arguing about books you don't really know. You should always assess the power wielded by the person you are talking to.

A friend of a friend, a brilliant person with a silver tongue, applied to a grand old university to study English and History. At interview he was, unsurprisingly, asked to talk about the relationship between the two disciplines. Could he think of a text that was particularly valuable as both literature and historical source material? He mentioned the Icelandic sagas, citing their combination of a strikingly economical style and a distillation of history; they had literary appeal, but were also valuable sources of knowledge about voyages and patterns of migration. His interviewer, evidently surprised to find a seventeen-year-old enthused by what he called 'these remote epics', asked what he most liked about them. 'I enjoy the power of the verse,' my friend's friend explained. And here his story broke down. The Icelandic sagas are in prose, and contain just the odd snatch of poetry.

A quick word here about 'epic', because the term will recur. In essence, an epic is an account of extraordinary events, told in lofty poetic language. Epic literature tends to deal with incidents that are important in the construction of a culture or a nation. It is ambitious, and it is large, and it is concerned with heroism. Thus Homer's *Iliad* and *Odyssey* are considered epics, along with the Anglo-Saxon poem *Beowulf*, John Milton's *Paradise Lost* and – to give a modern example – *Omeros* by the Nobel Prize-winning poet Derek Walcott. Epic is usually dominated by male characters. By contrast, the Icelandic sagas pay plenty of attention to women, and they are about farmers, not kings. They are therefore said to be 'like epics', but not actually to be epics. One more reason they get excluded from the epic genre is this awkward business of their having been written as prose. My friend's friend was not offered a place at that august university.

Schadenfreude is not on the menu here, for his mistake is of a sort that we have all made. In trying to impress, we overreach. When I was a child I belonged to a film club. One of the other kids in the club, whom I'll call Matthew, would always scan the notice of forthcoming screenings and yawn: '*Waltzing Matilda*? Seen it. *The Spy Who Loved Me*? Seen it. *Kes*? Seen it.' Occasionally he would punctuate this incantation with a critical comment: 'It's amazing' or 'That one's shit.' One day the last item on the list was 'To Be Announced'. Matthew, true to form, skated down the list, dismissing each film as old news, and concluding, '*To Be Announced*. Seen it. It's shit.' His image collapsed in a gale of laughter.

The essential question for a person who wants to talk about films he hasn't seen or books she hasn't read would appear to be 'How much do you need to know to be able to get away with ignorance?' And there is a second important consideration . . .

How can you make a little learning go a very long way?

One of the reasons we are able to get away with pretending to have read books we've never even dipped into is that half the time the person we are seeking to impress hasn't read them either. This will probably not be true of that tortuous university interview – though, actually, convincing the world's leading expert on John Milton that you've got to grips with *Paradise Lost* may be quite easy; the more someone knows about a subject, the more accustomed they are to finding that others know less about it, and from the Olympian heights of academe the various shades of *less*ness can be hard to distinguish. To a scholar profoundly invested in a subject, the difference between a sixth-former who has read a book and one who hasn't can be imperceptible, since both are likely to seem fabulously ignorant.

What's more, a touch of worldliness does not go amiss when you are dealing with scholars. I once managed to satisfy an eminent academic that I knew a great deal about the philosopher Immanuel Kant simply by broaching the small matter of Kant's interest in the platypus. To this day I can't remember where I'd picked up the notion that Kant gave two hoots about the platypus. There is a book by Umberto Eco which, when it appeared in English, was given the title *Kant and the Platypus*, but that was in 1999, and my conversation with the eminent academic took place in 1996. (The connection Eco makes seems in any case capricious. 'What has Kant go to do with the platypus?' he writes. 'Nothing . . . And this should suffice to justify the title and its use'.) Thankfully, in 1996, while knowing little of either Kant or Eco, I did know a bit about the platypus, and it put me on much safer ground than any hokey attempt to explore Kant's radical ideas about categories and perceptual judgements. My distinguished interlocutor – a man so unworldly that he needed to have explained to him, when I told him I didn't have a garden because I lived in a flat, what a flat was – proved, to my amusement, flummoxed by my display of swagger. 'You clearly know far more about Kant than I do,' he said, without a trace of irony.

Most of us spend only a very small part of our lives fibbing our way through college interviews or bamboozling sages. But we've all blagged: tried to gain admission to a club or a party we definitely weren't meant to be at, or jumped a queue on some bogus pretext. What is the secret of blagging? Fundamentally, it involves fearlessness and charm. This is at once verbal and physical. And it is not simply something you 'do' to others; it is also something you do to yourself.

The majority of people don't have the time, the energy or perhaps the desire to carve their way through *War and Peace*. But they still want to know what it's about. Maybe they're like my friend the hedge-fund guru who makes a point of being *au fait* with the latest cool fiction so that he can impress women at drinks parties with his shtick (yes, I said *shtick*) about the most recent Philip Roth – or by enthusing about Virginia Woolf. Do I hear you say *yuck*? Is this behaviour really worse than any of the other means of social display?

There are, you should also be aware, books that no one reads, no matter what may be protested to the contrary. I know nobody who can honestly claim to have read *Finnegans Wake*, James Joyce's bewilderingly esoteric comedy set in a pub in a Dublin suburb. (There are doubtless people who have read it, but they are neither numerous nor for the most part socially visible.) I have started *Finnegans Wake* half a dozen times, but have never got further than around page 18 of my Penguin edition. Perhaps it is just the book's opening that is difficult? But no, I have checked, flipping to the centre of my embarrassingly crisp-looking copy. It's still as hard as bench-pressing a grizzly bear. When Ezra Pound, a poet whose own works could hardly be described as straightforward, was asked what he made of *Finnegans Wake*, he suggested that the only justification for reading it would be if the experience could cure venereal disease. Joyce's own brother Stanislaus dubbed it 'an incomprehensible night-book'. Nevertheless, I've found that the knowledge that in *Finnegans Wake* Joyce writes the punning words 'when they were yung and easily freudened' can be made to go a surprisingly long way.

A related class of books consists of those read exclusively by literature students and the people who teach them. The classic example, still compulsory at some universities, is *The Faerie Queene*, Edmund Spenser's allegorical sixteenth-century epic promoting different types of virtue. One of the more humane people I know is a Spenser scholar, yet even he, in a list of his favourite reading, adds a parenthetical *ahem* after mentioning *The Faerie Queene*. My own approach to reading this daunting production was to sit it on my lap while watching Test cricket on TV: I would gulp a stanza (nine lines) between deliveries.

Four books almost no one has actually read

1. John Bunyan, *The Pilgrim's Progress*. In the more than 300 years since its publication, this Christian allegory has never been out of print, but today it is read by few for its theological content and by even fewer for pleasure.

2. Adolf Hitler, *Mein Kampf*. It's not hard to see why this mix of autobiography and political treatise isn't widely consumed any more, but how many of the millions who elected Hitler to power troubled to read it either?

3. Robert Burton, *The Anatomy of Melancholy*. An unclassifiable book which combines medicine, theology, psychology, philosophy and plenty besides. It is often held up as a marvel of English literature and a work of delightful eccentricity, but there are far more people who talk about it than have read a whole page of its contents.

4. Robert Musil, *The Man Without Qualities*. Now frequently acclaimed as one of the three greatest novels of the twentieth century, along with James Joyce's *Ulysses* and Marcel Proust's *À la recherche du temps perdu*, this vast book is spoken of far, far more often that it is even picked up.

This meant I could get through more than 500 stanzas a day, and the six completed books of Spenser's epic took me half a Test series. When I got to the end, I was challenged by a friend to quote a single line. I could quote one: 'A gentle knight was pricking on the plain.' The first.

Perhaps I exaggerate a little, but what this illustrates is that sometimes the fruits of actually reading a book are not tangible. My approach to reading *The Faerie Queene* was no doubt flawed, but I did read it, and I invested a good deal of time in doing so. By the time I finished it, I had a clear impression of what it was like, but I could have achieved this by dipping into it and probably even by just reading about it. This suspicion was confirmed when my college tutor applauded the response to Spenser's poem of a fellow student who had not read a single word of it.

In any case, most people are too polite to tell you when you're talking baloney. One of the reasons for this is that many people who really do have an idea what they are talking about sound as though they don't. Consider, for instance, this sentence, which follows a discussion of a scene in a film by Jean-Luc Godard: 'It is the moment of non-construction, disclosing the absentation of actuality from the concept in part through its invitation to emphasize, in reading, the helplessness – rather than the will to power – of its fall into conceptuality.' I have not made this up. These words are taken from Paul Fry's *A Defense of Poetry*, published by the wholly respectable Stanford University Press in 1995. Mr Fry is a professor at Yale. A crude but useful rule in all matters of the intellect is that if you cannot explain something simply you probably don't understand it quite as well as you imagine. An additional rule, a paradigm for chancers, is that if you know you don't understand something you should ape the experts and not really *explain* it at all.

Where's *this* book coming from, anyway?

At this point I should make clear that the idea for the book you have before you is not original. The germ of it existed in my mind a long time ago, but its development was inspired by my reading Pierre Bayard's *Comment parler des livres que l'on n'a pas lus?* (2007), which also mentions Lodge's game 'Humiliation'. Bayard's thesis is an intriguing one. 'Most statements about a book are not about the book itself, despite appearances,' he claims, 'but about the larger set of books on which our culture depends at that moment.' What is at stake in all our conversations about books, then, is 'our mastery of this collective library' – 'a command of relations, not of any book in isolation', which 'easily accommodates ignorance of a large part of the whole'. Thus knowing what genre a book belongs to can help us judge it without having read it; we understand where it stands. Furthermore, the difference between reading and not reading is, he says, narrower than we are accustomed to think. You could, for instance, remember reading Victor Hugo's *Les Misérables* and crying hopelessly over the sad bits, but if you cannot actually remember what those sad bits were, and if you cannot really recall what the book was about, can you honestly claim to know more about it than someone who has not read it at all? And are you in fact in any better a position than that person?

Bayard argues that we should not feel ashamed about what we have not read. But then, as the novelist Hilary Mantel pointed out in her review of the English translation of Bayard's book, the British seldom do. 'Outside academe,' she wrote, 'the average Briton is inclined to boast about what he has not read. Faced with the author in person, the Briton says scathingly, "Never heard of you," sometimes adding, "My wife reads – perhaps she's heard of you."' In a manner every bit as shameless, many of Mantel's fellow reviewers cracked the joke that they had arrived at their opinions of Bayard's book without having read it.

I don't think feeling ashamed of literary ignorance is uniquely French, but Bayard's *Comment parler?* is Gallic to the core – which is to say unapologetically abstract and philosophical, as well as steeped in references to Proust, Balzac and Paul Valéry (the last of these a 'master of non-reading'). It conjures an image of Gauloise-toting sages sitting in Les Deux Magots or Le Flore, pinballing argument and counter-argument off dinky glasses of pastis.

Bayard suggests that sometimes when talking of a book one has not read it is wise to be enthusiastic – even gushingly so. I disagree. Among the English insincere enthusiasm is easily spotted. Much better to be scathing or at least sceptical. There is a saying 'Never praise one Irish writer to another.' (W. B. Yeats advised his fellow Irish poets to learn their trade and 'Scorn the sort now growing up / All out of shape from toe to top.') Praise, especially when it feels vacuous, has a capacity for provoking questions and counter-arguments much more pungent than those summoned up by boldly phrased criticism.

However, condemnation needs to be meted out in the correct critical idiom. To describe a book or a writer as 'prosaic' is far more damning and altogether more convincing than to refer to him or it as 'dull'. A particularly unanswerable criticism is to say that you think something is 'deliberately' bad. You can be diversionary and elliptical, zig-zagging from one topic to another, conjuring a smokescreen of sophistry. But vagueness is not recommended. Anyone can generalize; as the poet William Blake argued, it is 'minute particulars' that are the articles of genius, and the constituents of skilful dissimulation are snippets of detail.

My take on the question of how to talk about books you haven't read is a concrete one. It is concerned with particular books and authors that we are often expected to know about, and it is concerned with real strategies for dealing with the holes in our knowledge. While I do include a few plot sum-maries and boil-in-the-bag opinions, these are easy enough to find elsewhere: instead what you have in your hands is, I hope, something more piquant and provocative.

Instead of adopting a chronological approach or inching my way through one genre before going on to the next, I want to move as conversation does – lubriciously, slipping from one enthusiasm to the next, making connections and leaving behind a few loose ends. A historical trudge from Greek tragedy to the present day isn't going to help you one jot. Better to move flexibly through the ages, without that kind of groggy predictability.

Let's begin with an author whose stock is high. On Facebook, the social networking website, there are groups with the titles 'I am going to marry one of the men in Jane Austen's novels,' 'Jane Austen books are ruining my sense of reality – and I love it!', 'Real men read Jane Austen' and 'I would invite Johnny Depp and Jane Austen to my dinner party.' You can learn a good deal about an author from her fans, but you can learn more from her enemies.

———————

What not to do in a university interview

Don't pretend to be immensely interested in the interviewer's specialist subject, which, if you're dealing with a literature expert, will be something terrifically arcane such as Swiss translations of the novels of Maria Edgeworth. Don't talk all the time, gabbling like a demented bird – or, worse, a TV evangelist. Don't wear any brand-new clothes that will cause you to resemble a Marks and Spencer mannequin. Don't for a moment convey the impression that you think you are more intelligent than the interviewer. Don't be chippy. Don't say any of the following: 'This suit has been in my family for four generations,' 'Name three things I'm not? Erm . . . interested . . . in . . . this,' 'I mainly want to come here because this place was built on a meadow where my grandfather used to graze his horses,' 'Do you mind if I skin up?' And don't allow yourself to be thrown by a strange question, such as 'Would people read Shakespeare in heaven?' Instead, gently nudge the discussion towards safe ground. But if the question is 'Why is the carpet in this room green?' consider replying 'Because little goblins creep in here at night and paint it that colour.'

———————

2

WOULD YOU INVITE JANE AUSTEN TO YOUR DINNER PARTY?

Jane Austen lived from 1775 to 1817.

Major works: her six novels, of which the most famous are *Pride and Prejudice* and *Emma*.

Also wrote: a short 'History of England', when she was fifteen. The manuscript, illustrated by her sister Cassandra, is just thirty-four pages long.

Trivia: two of her brothers, Francis and Charles, were admirals. During her lifetime, they were the ones who enjoyed large reputations; hers has been achieved since her death. She went to great lengths not to be identified as the author of her books, and not one of them was printed with her name on it in her lifetime.

In Britain it is not the norm for strangers to strike up conversation on public transport, unless it breaks down. When a stranger does accost you, it's probably because he or she is a foreigner or an oddball. Some years ago, I was sitting on the top deck of a number 94 bus, which was idling near Kensington Gardens, when a girl of about fifteen, dungareed and strangely coiffed, approached me, gestured at the book I was reading – Fanny Burney's *Evelina* – and announced, 'I'm glad you're not reading that total shit Jane Austen.' That, in the words of the pop song, was as far as the conversation went. But I was impressed. There are things you never expect to find next to one another: shit and Jane Austen are unlikely neighbours.

Austen is probably the most beloved of English novelists, yet also the most detested. For every 'Janeite' (female) who revels in her books' ladylike delicacy, there is an aggrieved sixth-former (male?) who has had to plod through *Mansfield Park* to pass a public exam. Both types of reader miss the essence of her work. The Janeite fails to see how urbane she is, and the aggrieved student is diverted by Assessment Objectives and other such drab considerations from the humour that is the lifeblood of Austen's writing. In their different ways, both seem to miss the seriousness of her vision.

Austen's name is most often invoked because of the film and TV adaptations of her novels. These elicit adoration and revulsion in roughly equal measures. There are plenty of men whose idea of a date from hell involves sitting at the local multiplex watching some new mangling of *Pride and Prejudice*. And there are plenty of people of both sexes who will recoil from the spectacle of Donald Sutherland and Brenda Blethyn somehow manacled together as that book's Mr and Mrs Bennet. But then there are those who are moved, to tears or to delirious laughter, by the sight of Mr Darcy emerging dripping wet after a dip in his lake – a scene that is most viewers' abiding memory of the 1995

BBC adaptation, in which, to quote *The Times*'s reviewer, Colin Firth's Darcy 'wore trousers so tight that you could count the small change in his pocket'. Opinions about these adaptations – and their number shows no sign of tailing off – lead into opinions about their fidelity to the original Austen texts, and then into opinions about the texts themselves. The most common debate is about which is the best of the novels. Often this comes down to an argument between *Pride and Prejudice* – recently voted Britain's favourite book, five places ahead of the Bible – and *Emma* – hailed by knowing readers as the greatest English fiction of its period. A small number of dissenting voices will argue for one of Austen's other four finished novels, with *Persuasion* the preserve of what sees itself as an especially discerning minority.

Many readers, men especially, are put off Jane Austen because, from what they can make out, she writes only about the little vicissitudes of family life. In Austen's novels, surely, nothing much happens? The characters seem forever to be agitating over whether they are to be invited to such and such a social event. Failing that, they play cards or musical instruments, and keep annoyingly quiet about their feelings. To many sceptics, they all seem rather like Henry Tilney in *Northanger Abbey*, who intones, 'Remember the country and the age in which we live. Remember that we are English, that we are Christians.' Remember to stay awake.

Moreover, Austen writes about a narrow section of society. 'I should hardly like to live with her ladies and gentlemen, in their elegant but confined houses,' avowed Charlotte Brontë in a letter to George Henry Lewes (later the companion of George Eliot). The essayist Ralph Waldo Emerson considered Austen 'sterile in artistic invention' and 'imprisoned in the wretched conventions of English society'. Even her keen admirer Sir Walter Scott could not avert the suspicion that she was a homely miniaturist, celebrating in her writing 'the exquisite touch which renders ordinary commonplace things and characters interesting'. To sceptics, her novels are like airless rooms with long but empty views.

Austen herself was to a large degree responsible for these opinions of her work. She referred to 'such pictures of domestic life in Country Villages as I deal in', and to her novels resembling the work done with a fine brush on a 'little bit (two inches wide) of ivory'. 'Three or four families in a Country Village' were enough material for a book. Yet these assessments are neither a limitation nor precisely true.

It is fair to say that Jane Austen's books do not obviously engage with the traumas of world events. If you go to them hoping to read about the battlefield and the depravities of the slave trade, you will be disappointed. (The impact of the Napoleonic Wars does figure in her novels, and it is not difficult to spot references to the sugar plantations of the Caribbean and to the changing structure of the British class system, but her stories are not really about these larger affairs.) For the most part, the novels are dramas of the familiar. Genteel manners are to the fore. The books' terrain is domestic. 'Marital, not martial,' as a wit might say – and probably has.

The shortage of specific references to contemporary happenings – the French Revolution, for instance – means that the books seem timeless; there is little that ties them to the period in which they were written. One of the paradoxes of the Janeite cult is that its celebrants, even as they rejoice in the bits of the novels about gowns and dancing and needlework, may easily imagine that the books are set at a time quite close to the present. This is why Austen has become part of the English heritage industry, along with Beatrix Potter, cheesy little water-colours, scones, 'tea shoppes' and decorative candles. She can be co-opted as a patron of rural living, the niceties of rank and hierarchy, the whole Tory notion of social order. A Christian, she equated virtue with happiness. She endorsed the idea of the nuclear family, and her books seem to argue for stability in the differing roles of men and women.

Because Austen's heroines aspire to get married, and because this is something they achieve, commentators have gone so far as to claim that her novels are an invaluable source of marital advice; her female characters are educated in how to get married and stay married, and so, it's argued, are her readers. One study, by the delightfully obscure novelist Beatrice Kean Seymour, claims, 'In a society which has enthroned the machine-gun . . . there will always be men and women . . . who will turn to her novels with an unending sense of relief and thankfulness.' This is probably true; many readers have found in Austen's world of good manners and polite visits a refreshing antidote to modern moral relativism. There used to be a bumper sticker you could buy which bore the legend 'I'd rather be reading Jane Austen': immersion in her books has struck generations of admirers as being preferable to the tired routines of real life – and to a lot of the gaudy things that are supposed to be its pleasures.

So where's the sting in Jane Austen?

This is only half the story, but it's the half that puts a lot of people off. The other half is less well known.

In my early twenties I worked part-time in a crammer, priming reluctant teenagers for their exams. One year I found myself teaching *Emma* to an eighteen-year-old boy, Mark, whose opening salvo when we met was 'I used to play football with Michael Owen. I was better than him and all.' I sensed this was not going to be an easy assignment. The problem was that Mark had up till then studied *Emma* in a class that had otherwise consisted of what he called 'daft girls'. They had cooed over the romantic entanglements. They had swooned at the thought of Frank Churchill, a man so modish he went to London merely to get a haircut. Mark thought Jane Austen was a petticoated airhead: *Emma* was the most boring thing in his world. I looked at him intently, and said something like this: 'The one thing you need to understand about Jane Austen is that she thinks people are . . . well, to put it bluntly, they're arseholes.' From that moment Mark and I were on more exciting ground.

My claim was a little over-egged. But it is a mistake to imagine that assemblies and cross-stitch and footling with bonnets are all there is to Jane Austen – to think that she blithely purveys romantic slush, or that she is sanctimonious and politely reverential of the gradations of the class system. Austen writes about her chosen milieu not because she is eager to endorse its values, but because it is something at which she knows she can excel.

Almost seventy years ago the psychologist D. W. Harding published an essay with the title 'Regulated Hatred: an aspect of Jane Austen'. Harding's phrase seems excessive, but Austen is supremely alert to the darkness of human motives, and she can be subversive. As Harding noted, 'her books are, as she meant them to be, read and enjoyed by precisely the sort of people she disliked', and 'she is a literary classic of the society which attitudes like hers, held widely enough, would undermine'. The 'comfortable' reader overlooks her 'astringencies'. These astringencies are less easily overlooked in her correspondence. In a letter to her sister Cassandra, for instance, she writes of a woman 'brought to bed yesterday of a dead child, some weeks before she expected, owing to a fright. I suppose she happened unawares to look at her husband.' In the novels she is less overt, but the piquancy is not too hard to pick up. And she is not averse to risqué images. For example, in *Mansfield Park* the lively Miss Crawford explains she has become familiar with a number of admirals: '*Rears* and *Vices*, I saw enough. Now, do not be suspecting me of a pun.' Try that out on a dyed-in-the-wool Janeite! Austen characters don't get raunchy like the women in *Sex and the City*, but they do share their interest in networking, the roles women are expected to fulfil, and most of all, desire.

To see how readily Austen can be misread, you don't have to look any further than the most celebrated sentence she ever wrote. This is the opening of *Pride and Prejudice*: 'It is a truth universally acknowledged, that a single man in possession of a good fortune must be in want of a wife.' Taken at face value, this is, according to your perspective, either mildly offensive or painfully twee. But it should not be taken at face value. The sentence is an aphorism, and aphorisms exist to be challenged; they are provocations, not solutions. The tone is light and amiable, but the content is not.

The words 'universally acknowledged' are the key. Almost coquettishly, they invite contradiction. Truths are true and don't need 'acknowledging'. If we understand 'truth' here as a synonym for 'conventional piece of wisdom', it is probably fair to say that few such truths are 'universally acknowledged', and this certainly isn't one of them. Young men in possession of good fortunes want many things far more than they want marriage. In fact, reverse the polarity and you are closer to the truth: for a woman of slender means there are compelling reasons for taking a husband. We learn that one character, Charlotte Lucas, sees doing so as a 'preservative from want': 'without thinking highly either of men or of matrimony, marriage had always been her object'. The more immediate truth is this: you should be awake to the possibility that a smartly formulated opening line is actually a rhetorical gambit – intended to impress the unwary, and in need of closer attention.

Emma opens in the same sort of way as *Pride and Prejudice*, with a deceptive sparkle: 'Emma Woodhouse, handsome, clever and rich, with a comfortable home and happy disposition, seemed to unite some of the best blessings of existence.' Read briskly, this sounds nauseatingly pleasant. But read it again; the key word is 'seemed'. So much literature educates us to recognize the gulf between appearance and reality, and whenever we see the verb *to seem* we should be on high alert. Are Emma's looks, cleverness and money enough to make her feel truly blessed? Do they lead those around her to think she is blessed? What hazards might there be in thinking of her in such terms? Should we perhaps be troubled by the description of her as 'handsome'? Does the adjective contain a hint of misgivings about Emma's femininity – or lack of it? Is it possible, for that matter, to see in the words 'comfortable home and happy disposition' a suggestion of complacency and cosseted smugness? Austen wants us to ask such questions, but not at the first pass.

The handsomeness, cleverness and richness help explain why *Emma* has been adapted for the screen so many times. Emma herself – in the novel a twenty-year-old with scintillating hazel eyes – has been played by Gwyneth Paltrow and Kate Beckinsale, as well as by Judy Campbell and Diana Fairfax. In Amy Heckerling's *Clueless* (1995), this very English figure is translated into Cher Horowitz, a Los Angeles high-school student. Alicia Silverstone brings kookiness to the role. But, in her voice-over commentary on her various slips, she preserves some of Emma Woodhouse's ironic self-awareness, even if it is hard to imagine a father in one of Austen's novels saying to an amorous young man, 'If anything happens to my daughter, I've got a .45 and a shovel. I doubt anybody would miss you.' In spirit, if not in language, *Clueless* is close to Austen, perceptive about the allure of the superficial, as well as about the manners and codes by which people live.

Why do people love *Pride and Prejudice* so much?

Elizabeth Bennet, the heroine of the novel Austen described as 'my own darling child', is like Emma Woodhouse a twenty-year-old. *Pride and Prejudice* was originally called 'First Impressions', and we all know about those: the disarmingly immediate appeal of a person or a car or a dress that later turns out to be trash; the sadly low estimate we make of something (a building, say) based on its exterior; the capacity of our initial judgements to influence our thoughts for ages afterwards.

At first Elizabeth is impressed, as others are, by the 'fine, tall person' and 'noble' looks of Mr Darcy (whose given name, preposterously, is Fitzwilliam), but she is not much taken with his manners. Darcy for his part says of Elizabeth, 'She is tolerable, but not handsome enough to tempt *me*.' Reflecting on Darcy's not having danced with her, Elizabeth says, 'I could easily forgive *his* pride, if he had not mortified *mine*.' Charlotte Lucas's young brother offers a different view: 'If I were as rich as Mr Darcy . . . I should not care how proud I was. I would keep a pack of foxhounds, and drink a bottle of wine a day.' The keynote here is not pride or prejudice – we're not being offered some sort of choice between them – but rather a combination of the two. It is necessary for both characters to relinquish some of their pride and some of their prejudice, and they do so because they have opportunities to do so. I doubt I am spoiling the plot if I say that Elizabeth ends up with Darcy. But it would be crass to say she *falls* in love with him. The process by which she becomes attracted to him is one of small adjustments.

While nursing her ambivalence about this handsome and apparently disagreeable man, Elizabeth receives an unwelcome offer of marriage from another quarter – Mr Collins, a clergyman with an enthusiasm for gardening. Even before we see Mr Collins, he has made an ass of himself with a letter which manages to be both fawning and self-important. On closer acquaintance, he does not get any better. The 'heavy-looking' Collins is a masterpiece of charmless and presumptuous formality. When he dines with the Bennets for this first time, he irks Elizabeth's mother by imagining that the meal has been prepared by one of her daughters. Mrs Bennet explains that her family is 'very well able to keep a good cook'. Mr Collins 'begged pardon for having displeased her. In a softened tone she declared herself not at all offended; but he continued to apologize for about a quarter of an hour.' Later, he proposes to Elizabeth, assuring her 'in the most animated language of the violence of my affection'. The speech, which is long and brilliantly conceived by Austen (though not by Mr Collins), has to be read in its entirety, but the highlight is its conclusion. The grotesque young clergyman explains:

> To fortune I am perfectly indifferent, and shall make no demand of that nature on your father, since I am well aware it could not be complied with; and that one thousand pounds in the four per cents, which will not be yours till after your mother's decease, is all that you may ever be entitled to. On that head, therefore, I shall be uniformly silent; and you may assure yourself that no ungenerous reproach shall ever pass my lips when we are married.

Elizabeth's reaction need not be spelt out here. Suffice it to say that she finds Mr Collins wildly absurd. And he continues to invite mirth, telling her that 'your refusal of my addresses is merely words of course': 'As I must therefore conclude that you are not serious in your rejection of me, I shall choose to attribute it to your wish of increasing my love by suspense.' It is worth remembering that he is twenty-five, for surely it is a young man's blunder to think that rejection is really an elegant form of acceptance.

Charlotte Lucas, who is twenty-seven (old to be single in Austen's society), takes a different view from Elizabeth. When Mr Collins's affections miraculously change their course, she acts quickly. She knows that she may never again be paid the compliment of a marriage proposal. For a moment we see things from her point of view. 'Mr Collins, to be sure, was neither sensible nor agreeable,' she reflects, and 'his society was irksome'. Therefore 'his attachment to her must be imaginary'. The reader has been beautifully wrong-footed here; the next sentence is 'But still he would be her husband.' Charlotte accepts Mr Collins 'solely from the pure and disinterested desire of an establishment'. Later, when we return to Elizabeth's point of view, we feel a touch embarrassed by her hasty insistence that Charlotte's engagement to such a man is 'impossible'.

Jane Austen, money and misreading

As we can see, Jane Austen is an acute observer of the calculations, miscalculations and corrections that are made in the name of love and of matrimony. Money always has a part in these calculations, and matters a great deal in her novels. For instance, Emma has £30,000 to her name, while Mr Darcy's country estate Pemberley brings in £10,000 a year. To put some perspective on this, in 1800 an income of £500 a year was considered better than adequate for a genteel single woman, while Austen's father felt able to invest in a carriage when his income rose to £700 a year, though he soon found he had to give it up as it was too costly. One of the reasons marriage matters so much in her world is that it gives women access to capital, or at least to the security that capital can provide. For Austen, who never married, it was important to make money out of her writing. Most authors feel that way, but there is an enduring image of Austen as someone above such mucky considerations. So consider this, from a letter to her brother Francis in the summer of 1813: 'You will be glad to hear that every copy of S. & S. is sold . . . I have now therefore written myself into £250 – which only makes me long for more.'

'S. & S.' is of course *Sense and Sensibility*, the first of Jane Austen's novels to be published, and one which is to an almost alarming degree about money. The story revolves around two contrasting sisters, Elinor and Marianne Dashwood. Elinor is capable of controlling her feelings: Marianne seems to think it would be wrong to do so. After first parting from Willoughby, the elusive gallant who helps her when she twists her ankle while out walking, Marianne 'would have thought herself very inexcusable had she been able to sleep at all'. To be composed at such a time is disgraceful in her eyes. Rather, 'she would have been ashamed to look her family in the face the next morning, had she not risen from her bed in more need of repose than when she lay down in it'. Her theatrical suffering is all too familiar to us. So is her concern about the weather. 'Observing the direction of the wind, watching the variations of the sky and imagining an alteration in the air', she appears the quintessential English weather-watcher, attentive to the elements' capacity to shape one's mood and actions. But even Marianne is alive to the importance of money. She craves the spending power of a man with £2,000 a year. While her sister is shocked, for half that amount is her idea of real wealth, Marianne has clearly thought the matter through: 'A proper establishment of servants, a carriage, perhaps two, and hunters, cannot be supported on less.' This all sounds mercenary – and more than a little like a conversation you might today overhear at lunch in a painfully fashionable restaurant. It is certainly relevant that the man with whom Marianne ends up, Colonel Brandon, has

£2,000 a year. After all, the three Dashwood girls and their mother have had but £500 a year between them. Austen knew all about the amorous effects of wealth: as the opening sentence of *Pride and Prejudice* slipperily suggests, a single man in possession of a good fortune will not find it hard to bag himself a wife.

In *Northanger Abbey*, the first novel Austen completed, we see the same sort of thing. A young man getting married is presented with a living worth £400 a year, which is enough for a couple starting out, though not sufficient to satisfy his bride, who unconvincingly declares the amount 'very charming indeed', despite her earlier assertions that 'where people are really attached, poverty itself is wealth' and 'the smallest income in nature would be enough for me'. However, the most distinctive feature of this book is its picture of the dangers of setting too much store by fiction. Its heroine, Catherine Morland, reads for pleasure, yet also so as to belong. Novels, as Austen pleads intrusively, are vessels 'in which the most thorough knowledge of human nature, the happiest delineation of its varieties, the liveliest effusions of wit and humour, are conveyed to the world in the best-chosen language'. Nevertheless, their power can produce uncanny and unhealthy effects. Dr Johnson, a strong influence on Austen, argued that 'they are the entertainment of minds unfurnished with ideas, and therefore easily susceptible of impressions'. Catherine is just the sort of person he was imagining.

Northanger Abbey is a book about misreading, and it demands a keen attention to detail on the part of the reader. We see this early on, when Catherine's father is described as being 'a very respectable man, though his name was Richard'. If we are being suitably alert, we ought to be surprised by that 'though';

apparently the Austen family had a strange prejudice against the name. The people Catherine meets also need deciphering. She escapes her banal home life when she is taken to Bath, and there the competitors for her affections are Henry Tilney, a clergyman in his mid-twenties, and John Thorpe, a stout and buffoonish Oxford undergraduate. Thorpe seems easily evaluated, as he brags about his 'well hung' carriage and refers to both Henry's father and Catherine's neighbour Mr Allen as being 'rich as a Jew'. Henry is harder to make out. Early on, for instance, he shows that he knows a good deal about fabrics, commenting on the prices of different kinds of muslin, and observing of Catherine's gown that its 'very pretty' material is likely to fray. Catherine is startled. This isn't the sort of thing young men are meant to know about. Austen writes, ' "How can you," said Catherine, laughing, "be so —" She had almost said "strange".' She doesn't get the word out, which is just as well; for her to be so impertinent as to say this would actually be stranger than for Henry to know about muslin. Her restraint pays off: Henry will turn out in other, more interesting ways to differ from her accustomed idea of men. Reading has provided her with certain types and categories, ways of understanding the world. These can be useful, but, as she discovers, they can stifle her perceptions.

The novel offers some useful sidelights on social history in its account of the different reading habits of men and women. Men, it seems, read quickly and alone, favour newspapers, and rarely read novels, though John Thorpe has got through Henry Fielding's *Tom Jones* and Matthew Lewis's *The Monk* – the latter a sensational work which features both rape and incest. He is a cautionary example of the person who talks about books he has not read, slating *The Mysteries of Udolpho* and saying that he much prefers the work of Anne Radcliffe – who is, unfortunately, the author of that very novel. By contrast, the women in *Northanger Abbey* are sociable readers, sharing books, and they openly prefer fiction. For Catherine the trouble comes when ideas drawn from her reading of novels seep, unnoticed, into other areas of her life. She sees mysteries where there are none. Innocent matters appear sinister, because she is used to stories full of macabre exaggeration. It falls to Henry to counsel her, 'Consult your own understanding, your own sense of the probable, your own observation of what is passing around you.' Imagination, she learns, needs to be balanced by reason and experience.

As Catherine Morland's naive adventures illustrate, Austen's heroines do not fit conventional ideas of the heroic. For instance, the principal character in *Mansfield Park*, Fanny Price, is a strange creature – quiet, blushing, pallid, sickly, 'puny', possibly anaemic, definitely hypersensitive, emotionally intelligent, possessed of a 'sweet smile', delighted to be left to her own devices, and keen on reading serious-minded essays that promise to be morally improving. She *does* next to nothing.

In Austen's last finished work, *Persuasion*, the role of unemphatic heroine belongs to Anne Elliot, who is older (twenty-seven, like Charlotte Lucas): she has a certain prettiness, but 'her bloom had vanished early', and she has slipped into depressive silence and languid insignificance. At the outset we are told that 'her word had no weight' and 'her convenience was always to give way'; her 'usual fate' consists of being required to do 'something very opposite from her inclination'. As Anne's story unfurls, she becomes more articulate, but she and Fanny Price both embody the idea that one can indirectly be expressive – that a person can be passive and still be powerful. Silence can be used to achieve control. When Anne and Fanny are eventually proposed to by the men they favour, the question is one these quiet heroines have already asked through their actions, though not through their words. Triumph's tune can be played at low volume.

Marriages in Jane Austen's novels (with the likely ages, at the point where they marry, of those involved)

Northanger Abbey: Catherine Morland (18) and Henry Tilney (26)

Sense and Sensibility: Elinor Dashwood (20) and Edward Ferrars (24), Marianne Dashwood (19) and Colonel Brandon (37)

Emma: Emma Woodhouse (21) and George Knightley (38)

Pride and Prejudice: Elizabeth Bennet (21) and Fitzwilliam Darcy (28)

Mansfield Park: Fanny Price (18) and Edmund Bertram (24)

Persuasion: Anne Elliot (27) and Frederick Wentworth (31)

Triumph in all the novels means marriage. It is an institution which Austen supports, although she shows that in practice it can often be a miserable prison-house. This is why it is so important for each of her heroines to marry the right man. Marriage to him will be individual, not institutional, and will involve a minimum of sacrifice and a maximum of real attraction. One of the things that invariably happen in Austen's books is that her heroines become more perceptive about who and what this 'right' man should be. They learn to see, and learn, like Emma, to 'catch and comprehend the exact truth of the whole'. And all the while Austen sheds light on the complacency with which so many others seek and conduct relationships, as well as their habits of meddling, taking grotesque pleasure in the little misadventures of their acquaintances, and miring themselves in snobbery.

But isn't Austen all about dances and dandies?

A recurring setpiece in the novels, where both complacency and perceptiveness are much in evidence, is some sort of public event – typically, a ball. Some people will find this enough to put them off Austen completely. Aren't balls ludicrous? Surely they are nothing more than parades of smug elitism? I think the most useful thing I've ever read about formal occasions of this kind is Tony Tanner's observation, in his fine book on Austen, that 'Society forgathers to see how society forgathers.' People come together for these occasions with the intention of having fun, but of far greater importance is the drama of manners such occasions present. A party is a form of theatre, and the smarter its character the more theatrical it is designed to be. Guests perform the rituals of their class; they are watched as they do so, and watch others doing likewise. They parade accomplishments, evaluate each other, and form temporary alliances based on a shared awareness of other people's shortcomings. Jane Austen's works are lit up by this awareness that

41

social events are performances, and her attention to the subtleties of these performances is finely tuned. In truth, society itself is a fiction.

This is what makes Austen intriguing: the blend of subversiveness and conventionality. Or, to put it another way, readers of her novels continually find themselves thinking 'Is she a conservative . . . or something else?' How conscious is she of her art? How in tune with the spirit of her age? Partly because her 'philosophy of life' and her attitudes are hard to pin down, we don't often hear that something is 'Austenian'. (The exception is irony: 'cool', 'subtle', 'mild', 'exquisite' Austenian irony.) I suspect in fact this is because moments that are 'like Austen' are like something else: life.

In Karen Joy Fowler's *The Jane Austen Book Club* (2004) a group of six Austen enthusiasts – five women and a man – meet once a month to discuss, in turn, her six finished novels. 'Each of us has a private Austen,' the novel begins. And so it proves; every character is distinctly proprietary about her (or, in the one case, his) understanding of Austen. Thus Allegra, a glamorous lesbian artist, wonders if Charlotte Lucas in *Pride and Prejudice* might be gay. Her mother Sylvia reflects on this: 'Are you saying Austen meant her to be gay? Or that she's gay and Austen doesn't know it?'

As Karen Joy Fowler's novel emphasizes, Austen's are books that people go back to, again and again. Each reading discloses new details. When we return to a book we think we know well – or to a favourite film, or indeed to a memory – we are often surprised by how different it is from how we remembered it. Perhaps we have changed, or maybe we are simply in a different sort of mood; but then again, perhaps our previous reading of the book was quick, lazy, imprecise, unscrupulous – or, conversely, hypersensitive, too earnest, too vigilant to be pleasurable. The best books appear inexhaustible. One of the things that Austen's books show us convincingly is that there are different approaches to making sense of literature. This is what great writers do: they invent new ways of reading. To see this from two different angles, I want to turn first to the greatest authors of Latin and Greek and then to one of the most daunting of the twentieth century.

How to flummox a Janeite

The 'regulated hatred' angle will work a treat. After all, Janeites don't want to hear about that sort of thing, because it's the opposite of what they adore in their heroine's writing.

You could also try saying that Austen's unfinished novel *Sanditon*, with which she was busy in the final months of her life, represented a new direction for her – instead of the supposedly 'autumnal' shades of *Persuasion* we get biting satire, with Austen vigorously mocking her age's infatuation with commodities (including novels). Or you could poke fun at the very idea of literary cults.

Most bemusingly of all, you could cite the American scholar Claudia Johnson's defence of Janeites. Johnson argues that Janeites have, like ardent fans of *Star Trek*, been 'derided and marginalized by dominant cultural institutions bent on legitimizing their own . . . protocols of expertise'. What she means is that people who are rude about Janeites are snobs intent on making their own ways of reading look credible. Somehow this association between Austenland and the world of Mr Spock doesn't strike me as one that many lovers of *Pride and Prejudice* are going to cherish.

3

SPEAKING WITH THE DEAD: VIRGIL AND HOMER, LATIN AND GREEK

Major works: the *Iliad* and the *Odyssey* (Homer), the *Aeneid* (Virgil).

Also important: too many to mention, but among the big hitters are the Greek dramatists Aeschylus (difficult), Euripides (funnier) and Sophocles (known especially for the three Theban plays about Oedipus and, later, his daughter Antigone, who is also his half-sister), as well as the Latin poets Ovid (author of the *Metamorphoses*) and Horace (known mainly for his *Odes*).

Not long ago I found myself arguing with a (younger) writer about his unwillingness to read any contemporary fiction. 'I haven't read Philip Roth because I don't want to,' he insisted. 'I *know* I don't want to. I'd rather read Homer.' This, it seems to me, is unlikely to become a bumper-sticker legend.

I probably ought to explain straight away that, before sitting down to write this chapter, I hadn't read a word of Homer since my teens. I 'did' Book IX of the *Odyssey* aged fifteen, and made a fool of myself in front of my peers declaiming at ridiculous volume a section in which the Cyclops roars in agony after having a spear driven into his eye. So, while I could recall enjoying Homer, I was a mite sceptical that someone who liked sitting around drinking vanilla lattes was really going to give a large chunk of his leisure time over to stories of vengeance, human frailty, deception and divine ritual in Troy and Ithaca, Phaeacia and Sparta. But now, even if I have not changed my mind about the unlikelihood of Homer becoming a touchstone for addicts of flavoured coffee, my impressions have been refreshed. Dipping into Homer again in English, I feel a little as Keats did when he wrote of the same experience: 'like some watcher of the skies / When a new planet swims into his ken'.

In a moment I'll come back to what happens on Planet Homer, and to what I should have said to Mr Vanilla Latte. But first, an observation: the pre-eminent authors in Latin and Greek come up disarmingly often. It is not a freak occurrence to be thrown by a casual reference to Plato or Sophocles. Enemies of the Classics claim these authors have no relevance, but Latin and Greek are visibly embedded in English-speakers' culture, aesthetics and history. The contributions of the Latin and Greek civilizations to the English language are especially obvious. The argument that they are irrelevant leads in the end, pathetically, to the belief that there is nothing to be gained from studying the past or from engaging intellectually and imaginatively with what is alien to us.

The decline of Latin and Greek has, over a couple of generations, filled acres of newspaper. It is taken as melancholy evidence of the closing of the Western mind, a sign of the dwindling willingness to look hard and philosophically at the world. Latin and Greek are seen as victims of utilitarianism – swept aside because of the modern fixation with what's materially advantageous, squeezed out of the national curriculum by lessons in citizenship and condom use. There are plenty of people who see this as a very good thing. According to the journalist Neal Ascherson, writing back in 1991, 'Latin is part of England's fake heritage, part of that pseudo-ancient landscape which I call Druidic.' It has become no more than 'the private code of a privileged class', best allowed to crumble. We'll see about that.

Half-a-dozen Latin tags worth knowing

1. *sine qua non*. Used of something one cannot do without. Literally it means 'without which not'. Thus 'A silly jumper is a *sine qua non* for golfers.'
2. *ad hominem*. Literally 'to the man'. An attack *ad hominem* finds fault with a person rather than his arguments.
3. *mutatis mutandis*. 'Once the things that need changing have been changed' or, more succinctly, 'After all necessary changes'.
4. *pro tempore*. 'For the time being'. Usually abbreviated to *pro tem*, as in 'Let's accept *pro tem* her eligibility for this position.'
5. *per se*. 'In and of itself'. For example, 'Using Latin tags isn't an odious practice *per se*.'
6. *pro bono*. This is an abbreviation of *pro bono publico*, meaning 'for the public good'. Someone operating *pro bono* does work of professional quality, but without payment.

The use of Classical tags and phrases is the kind of thing that gets Latin and Greek a bad name. It is now acceptable only among ageing barristers and effete art historians. We all use 'et cetera', and references to 'hoi polloi' (or, more often, and shoddily, 'the hoi polloi') are embarrassingly common, but only an eccentric could expect many people to know or care what he means – and yes, it will always be a *he* – when he slips into conversation the words 'sub specie aeternitatis'. If you find yourself talking about books you haven't read with someone who says 'sub specie aeternitatis', try and avoid anything Classical or even classic: you will be rumbled.

When I was a muddy-kneed pre-pubescent, being fed this 'private code of a privileged class', there was a song still quite popular among children who were cheerfully miserable about being force-fed Classics at school: 'Latin is a dead language, / Dead as dead can be. / First it killed the Romans, / And now it's killing me.' But Latin's deadness is debatable. There are a surprising number of people who may remember at some inappropriate moment that *fornix* is the Latin for an arch, and even a fair few who'll recall that Catullus in one of his poems writes '*quod culus tibi purior salillo est / nec toto decies cacas in anno*' ('Because your arse is purer than a salt-cellar, / You only take a shit ten times a year'). Reference to a 'cohort' – a vogue word of late – will irritate someone who knows that a Roman cohort contained precisely 480 men, divided into three 'manciples' of 160 each. These are small things, but in other, distinctive ways Latin, even though a language of the past, lives on: in inscriptions and mottoes (such as that of the European Union, *In varietate concordia*), in the Roman Catholic Church, in borrowed words and branches of science, and in some frequently visited quarters of the internet, as well as in the spells pronounced in the Harry Potter novels, on Angelina Jolie's stomach, and even on the radio in Finland, where there are weekly broadcasts in this reportedly defunct tongue. Here the dead can speak to the living, as they can in the writings of Virgil or Ovid.

If one stereotype of Latin and Greek is that they provide the privileged classes with a private code – though how much Latin or Greek would I actually hear if I dropped in at Glyndebourne, Cowdray Park, the Henley Regatta or the Chelsea Flower Show? – another is that people who have a knowledge of these languages are intelligent, serious-minded, systematic thinkers, possessed of an enviably rare skill. The school of snobbery to which Latin and Greek appeal is intellectual rather than social. Latin and Greek are luxuries of the mind, and their authors can seem thrillingly resistant to the empty seductions of convenience and 'usefulness'.

Really ludicrous people will profess enthusiasm for Sappho – even though only tiny fragments of her poetry survive – or Quintilian, author of a giant textbook on rhetoric that was among the favourite reading of Martin Luther. Dangerously highbrow types will talk up Lucretius, whose *De rerum natura* is a poetic masterpiece which combines some hardcore physics with a recipe for managing one's experience of pleasure and pain. The pre-Socratic philosophers are a favourite of playfully donnish types, mainly on account of their nuggety aphorisms and willingness to ask big questions like 'Where does everything come from?' and 'What is real?' The pick of them has to be Heraclitus, whose fearless assertions include 'Everything flows,' 'The way up and the way down are one and the same' and 'You cannot step into the same river twice' – this last because when you step into it the second time, the water's different, and so are you. This calls to mind an observation made by the critic Edmund Wilson, apposite here: 'No two persons ever read the same book.'

What does it mean to say something is 'Homeric' or 'Platonic'?

For all the appeal of these curious figures, it is the names Homer and Plato which come up most, often cast as adjectives. 'Homeric' seems to mean imposing, grand, dramatic, large-scale – in short, epic; 'Platonic' to mean pure, non-sexual, lofty, abstract, ideal. Plato's name is usually encountered in references to Platonic love and Platonic ideals. Platonic love is, for every-day purposes, a companionship that does not involve sex – my spiritual affection for a female friend, or what's sometimes known, rather more dodgily, as a romantic friendship. This is not what Plato had in mind. I'll explain what he did have in mind in a moment, through an account of Platonic ideals. But first, a quick word about Plato himself.

The philosopher's real name was Aristocles, and he earned his nickname on account of his sturdy build (*platon* meant 'broad-shouldered'). He lived for about eighty years in the fourth and fifth centuries BC, studied under Socrates, and founded the Athenian Academy, which was a forerunner of the modern university. It is not terribly controversial to say that he invented philosophy as we know it – although a bit more chancy to mention that he appears also to have invented a primitive alarm clock – and one not wholly jokey line that sometimes gets trotted out is that the European philosophy of the past two millennia has really just been a series of footnotes to Plato's writings. But it might be more accurate to say that Plato, fashions being what they are, is now mainly to be found in the footnotes. He's someone you refer to as though talking over your (not so broad) shoulder, turning your back on an argument that has gone flat: 'Of course, Plato says artists don't understand what they create . . .'

Still, if you are a chatty type, Plato is your kind of philosopher. Almost all his works take the form of a dialogue, because of his view that discussion – argument in speech – leads to considered, tested thought. Plato learnt from Socrates that the search for truth lasts all one's life and involves asking questions. One of his key works is the *Symposium*, which is set at a smart dinner party. There are seven people present; among them Socrates, the comic playwright Aristophanes, and a legal expert, Pausanias. The guests talk about love. Socrates says that love is a state of mind revealing our craving for happiness, a desire for a lasting ownership of beauty, and that it is best expressed through the soul rather than the body. Indeed, there is a ladder of love: on the first rung is physical attraction, and then comes intellectual attraction, and so on. The highest kind of love lies in contemplating 'the form of beauty'. To put it another way, pursuing a true understanding of beauty, rather than pursuing a person, is the ultimate expression of love. Part of the appeal of Plato's works is that they are full of claims with which one really wants to disagree, and here is an example. The *Symposium* doesn't really show us the essence of love and beauty; instead it encourages readers to keep searching for them. Rather attractively for those thinking about keeping the search alive, modern scholarly symposia often seem to happen in places such as California and Hawaii.

One of Plato's most fetching ideas, developed in *The Republic*, was that the reality we see all around us is a facsimile of a higher truth. I'm writing this sitting at a desk, and I'm fond of the desk, which is scarred with coffee rings. But this specific desk is, according to Plato, an imperfect representation of the ideal desk. My desk is 'material': the 'ideal' desk is abstract and eternal. The material world is illusory and changeable. This does not mean that everything around us is a dream, but rather that the world as we believe we know it is not a proper object of knowledge. Philosophers, who can see the essentials beneath the particulars, have knowledge: the rest of us have only beliefs.

In *The Republic* Plato offers the Parable of the Cave, which has a claim to be the most famous philosophical idea of all. Plato pictures a cave where ordinary people are held captive, able only to see its rear wall. Behind them is a fire, and between them and the fire there pass an assortment of objects – a bit like puppets. The prisoners can see the shadows of these things on the wall of the cave, but they cannot see the things themselves. This, says Plato, resembles everyday life: we are trapped inside illusions. But if the prisoners are released, they can ascend from the cave into a more enlightened state. This is what happens, according to Plato, when we cease to live in the shadow world of the senses. For a modern analogy, you might say that Plato's cave-dwellers resemble people who live their lives through television. They may be satisfied with what they see, but their powers of reason are not engaged.

Plato's writings are apt to leave readers with some work of their own to go away and do. The issues they address still command attention. But they are also very much 'of their time'. For instance, they are dotted with references to Homer, particularly the *Odyssey*. For Plato, as for his contemporaries, Homer was a cultural touchstone. Homer wasn't always generously treated, but he was deeply familiar; the bits of Homer used by Plato seem to be quoted from memory.

So who was Homer? It is not easy to say. Apparently a citizen of the eighth century BC, his name meant 'hostage', but beyond that nothing is certain. It is often stated that he was a blind minstrel, yet it has also been claimed that he was in fact a 'she', as well as that he was Odysseus himself, the child of Odysseus' son Telemachus or one of Penelope's lovers. In the end 'Homer', inasmuch as he is known, is a projection of the works he wrote – a convenient and intriguing idea.

Whether he was a woman or a minstrel, what did 'Homer' actually write?

Homer produced two poems. One is a traditional heroic epic of some 16,000 lines, the *Iliad*, which is aristocratic in subject matter – the power of royalty is taken for granted – and sophisticated in tone. A tragedy, it imagines the events of a few weeks in the tenth and final year of the siege of Troy, and is much concerned with combat, sacrifices, anger and insults. The Trojan War was sparked by lust; Paris, a Trojan, stole Helen, the wife of Menelaus, the King of Sparta. Menelaus' brother Agamemnon – memorably, in Christopher Logue's fine rendering of Homer, 'Cuntstruck Agamemnon' – raised an army to go to Troy and get her back. What followed, rather than being a blazing triumph, was a slow grind. The author assumes that we know this.

When the action of the *Iliad* gets under way, we see Agamemnon arguing with his leading warrior Achilles about how booty should be divided among the Greeks. The wrath of Achilles, set out in the poem's first four lines, impels its plot. Incensed by Agamemnon, Achilles withdraws from the war, with disastrous consequences for his countrymen; then, when his friend Patroclus is killed, he turns the full force of his anger on the Trojans, killing their prince Hector and desecrating his corpse. Half-man, half-god, Achilles is a warrior whose prowess has large effects, but he also represents the soldier traumatized by combat, driven to excess. At the heart of the *Iliad* is the question of what it means to be heroic. Achilles is impressive, yet imperfect. Today we tend to expect heroes to display moral excellence, but for the Greeks military excellence was sufficient to justify the name. Heroism did not mean flawless goodness, any more than it necessarily meant success.

Homer also produced a less stylised work, the *Odyssey*, which is about three-quarters the length of the *Iliad*. It focuses on one man, Odysseus, and his battle to return from the Trojan War to his home in Ithaca. More straightforwardly emotional than the *Iliad*, it covers a significantly longer time period. Odysseus's drawn-out wanderings are a quest, yet also an exploration of his own identity. (Quests, it could be argued, are always really about achieving self-knowledge.) Along the way he is tempted by the enchantress Circe and entrapped by the nymph Calypso. He descends into the underworld to speak with the blind prophet Tiresias, and he sees many of his companions eaten by the one-eyed giant Polyphemus, showered with rocks by giants, and finally destroyed by a thunderbolt. Odysseus is a fine athlete and navigator, a DIY whiz, a shrewd politician and a skilful orator, but he is also a liar and is far from perfect as a leader. In short, he is the sort of person who would kick butt in a reality TV show, and through him Homer again shows that it is possible to admire someone who is not wholly admirable.

Five great characters in Classical literature

1. Medea, who in Euripides' play of that name kills not only her faithless husband Jason's new bride, but also her own children by Jason.

2. Achilles in the *Iliad*. This mighty warrior has no control over his pride, and seems prepared to sacrifice anything in order to achieve the immortality of his reputation.

3. Dido in the *Aeneid*. The queen of Carthage, a capable ruler before Aeneas' arrival, is inflamed with something close to madness by her love for Aeneas. Her tumultuous passion is depicted in memorably physical terms – as a wound in her veins, for instance – and Aeneas' words are said to transfix her breast.

4. Aeschylus' Prometheus, a rebel and an intellectual who steals fire from Zeus and gives it to mortals. Whereas Zeus is portrayed as a tyrant hostile to humanity, Prometheus is the benefactor of mankind.

5. Orpheus in Ovid's *Metamorphoses*. Although he appears in only two of the work's fifteen books, this supreme singer is the model of a flawed artist transfigured by his artistic gifts. Tellingly, he is the inspiration for many of the first works of opera.

The two works are both concerned with human suffering, but they are strikingly different. The *Odyssey* revolves around one character, whereas the *Iliad* has no single presiding figure: the former is concerned with adventures and a personal mission, the latter with more broadly heroic values. Additionally, the *Odyssey*, unlike the *Iliad*, contains memorable female characters, shifts back and forward in time and setting, is overtly moral, and emphasizes the idea of justice. In the *Odyssey* the hero's weapon of choice is a bow and arrow; in the *Iliad* it is a spear. And so on, to the extent that for the past 300 years many scholars have suspected that the two works are the efforts of two separate poets.

Furthermore, they were intended for recitation, rather than for a reading public (there was no such thing, although it is wrong to think Homer's contemporaries were illiterate). As 'oral' texts, they were probably quite flexible, but in the form in which they survive to the present – written down, possibly at the request of the Athenian tyrant Peisistratus around 550 BC – they are static. The style of the poems is deliberately quite repetitious, and the poet makes generous use of what are known as formulaic epithets: a certain adjective will invariably attach to a particular character or object. Thus Odysseus is *polumetis* (ingenious, resourceful), the sea *oinopa* (dark as wine), and dawn *rhododactoulos* (rosy-fingered). Yet while Homer's vocabulary is repetitive, at the same time, paradoxically, his works contain numerous *hapax legomena*, words that appear just once. Only four times in the whole of Homer do a hundred lines pass without at least one such word being employed. For instance, there is *moiregenes*, a word meaning 'born with a favourable destiny', and *aoidimos*, meaning roughly 'suitable as a subject for song'. These aren't terms to start trying to adopt into daily speech, but the idea that some skills and situations call for a *hapax legomenon* is a nice one: not all the complexity of life has yet been put into words.

Moreover, and in the *Iliad* especially, there are contrived similes, many of them extended for far longer than a modern author would think viable. Thus in Book 11 of the *Iliad* the tussle between the Trojans and the Achaeans is described as being like what happens when two teams of reapers drive from opposite ends through a blessed man's field of wheat. And in Book 16 there is a moment where the Greeks pour out of their ships, scattering the Trojans, and a great noise rises up. We are told that the Greeks, as they save their ships from fire, are able for a moment to rest, and this – here I paraphrase – calls to mind the way in which the god Zeus moves a dense cloud away from crest of a great mountain, and suddenly reveals all the peaks, headlands and glades, and the sky opens, as though infinite.

Why should we care about Homer?

For some people, it is enough that we can call him the father of Greek literature, since on the strength of this one can say that Western literature begins with him. But not everyone will think this is sufficient. An alternative reason, then, is that his works embody certain specifically Greek values that might otherwise be eternally lost to us – ideas about the nobility of action, the importance of the supernatural, the cult of male friendship, and the dignity of dying young in combat. Others will argue that Europeans cannot make sense of themselves without a grasp of what their forebears thought and did, and that Homer's works embody an important part of that history. He can also be thought of as the precursor of science fiction and all our modern literature of violence. In the *Iliad*, he finds sixty different ways to say that characters die – a vocabulary of killing that shames modern purveyors of blood-spattered schlock – and we are told the names of more than 200 who do so.

Can we really understand him? His works test our powers of sympathy and historical imagination. For instance, when Odysseus is dubbed a 'Sacker of Cities', we might assume this is a criticism. In fact, it is praise. Victory in battle meant the expansion of one's civilization: defeat spelt its doom. The Homeric ideal of military excellence is of a warrior whose successes are complete; there must be nothing tentative about his achievement. This is something we may struggle to accept in a world where the Geneva Conventions hold force. Moreover, Homer's heroes are regal, whereas today's heroes tend to be ordinary troops – or fire-fighters, aid workers and activists. For Homer's heroes, justice equates to revenge. It's personal, not the work of institutions. Even if we identify with the desire for retribution, we have been culturally conditioned to resist it. Yet for all these differences, some things persist: the importance of courage, the veneration of athletes, and the hero's discovery that it is not easy to return home.

And why should we care about Virgil?

In many respects Virgil's *Aeneid* is modelled on Homer's two great poems, and it is an attempt to emulate them. The *Aeneid*'s episodic structure and epic language are inspired by Homer, and some of its incidents are reminiscences of things that happen in the *Iliad*. Furthermore, Virgil's poem begins with the words 'Arma virumque cano' ('I sing of arms and the man'), calling to mind both the military subject matter of the *Iliad* and the personal, individual focus of the *Odyssey*. The man in question is Aeneas, an ambiguous figure: civilized, urbane, and a symbol of the future magnificence of Rome, yet at times tired, indecisive and reserved. Where Odysseus was characterized as resourceful, Aeneas is characterized in terms of his respect for the gods, and in this the *Aeneid* is something different and new: one of its central concerns is responsibility, the sense of duty known to Romans as *pietas*. This *pietas*, usually directed towards the gods and one's family, formed part of a group of virtues esteemed in Roman society, including the readily identifiable *dignitas*, *industria* and *clementia*, plus one that has survived unchanged into English usage – *gravitas*. Gravitas is the weight of intellectual authority; it's something almost ceremonial, to be used against frivolity.

Unlike Homer, Virgil is an identifiable historical figure. Publius Vergilius Maro was born on 15 October in 70 BC near Mantua; he died on 21 September in 19 BC, in Naples. He wrote roughly 13,000 lines of poetry – not a large number for someone whose creative output spanned about twenty-five years. Besides the *Aeneid*, his notable achievements are the *Eclogues*, which in a witty yet also melancholy and politically charged style depicts the countryside as a sanctuary, and the *Georgics*, a patriotic evocation of the work of farming (divided into crops, trees, herd animals and bees), which argues the redemptive power of hard work and productivity, piety, modesty and tenacity.

I am not convinced that Virgil often comes up in conversation. When I was a child, a really harsh school punishment was to be made to copy out (in Latin) one of the *Georgics*. Somehow I can't imagine this happens very often now. My abiding memory of studying the *Aeneid*, meanwhile, is of one of my classmates asking our teacher, 'This "imagery" – what exactly is it?' The response was less than helpful: '*Imagery!?* Imagery is *imagery.*' It might have been kinder to explain that imagery is descriptive language which appeals to the reader's five senses in order to conjure up mental pictures. But kindness is not a word habitually associated with Latin teachers.

In the *Aeneid*, stunning images abound. Some survive translation. For instance, Aeneas at one point is described retreating from the fog of war in the same way that a ploughman runs from his field when a hailstorm begins. On another occasion King Latinus is put under considerable pressure by his belligerent subjects, and is described withstanding them every bit as solidly as a rock stands steadfast amid the roiling ocean's barking waves. Dido, Queen of Carthage, is pictured wounded by her desire for Aeneas, and we are told that she roams the city like an unwary hind which has been shot from far away by a hunter; the hunter does not know he has hit her, but she moves haphazardly in flight, the winged iron bolt all the while protruding from her flank. Elsewhere the souls of the dead are as numerous as the leaves that fall in a wood when autumn breathes its first chill, and a snake, hurled at Latinus's wife Amata by a Fury, seems to morph into a twisted golden torque about her neck and then into a ribbon holding her hair, as though her very jewels are alive.

While this is all strange, it is not overwhelmingly strange. When we read, it can be as though we have climbed inside another person's headspace, but what we find there, even in the literature of cultures far removed from our own, often looks surprisingly familiar. Amid all the archaism of the literature of Virgil and Homer, there is much that feels modern. In the *Odyssey*, for instance, Penelope displays a depth of intelligence that we might expect of a female character in a nineteenth-century novel, while Odysseus's organizational skills and focus on his goals have made him an unexpectedly useful point of reference for management gurus. To James Joyce, writing in the early part of the twentieth century, Homer's epic seemed that most reassuring type of production, a family drama. Besides being ripe for parody, it provided him with the perfect framework for a modern story of wanderings, homecoming and national character.

Two ways to wind up a Classicist

1. Say that on your way home from work you were set upon by hoodla, who had decided to flex their bicipites, but add that you were able to tidy yourself up merely by using several Kleenices, and that you then settled your nerves by drinking a martinus.

2. Start using risible Latin catchphrases, such as *Quid fit?* ('What's happening?'), *Hodie adsit, cras absit* ('Here today, gone tomorrow') and *Fac ut gaudeam* ('Make my day').

4

WHAT'S THE POINT OF *ULYSSES*?

James Joyce lived 1882–1941.

Major work: *Ulysses* (1922).

Also wrote: *Dubliners*, *A Portrait of the Artist as a Young Man*, *Finnegans Wake* (note that it does not have an apostrophe), poetry, and a play entitled *Exiles*.

Trivia: *Ulysses* is set on 16 June 1904, which was the day Joyce went on his first date with his future wife, Nora Barnacle. Each year 16 June, known as Bloomsday, is energetically celebrated by Joyce devotees in Dublin – and in several other communities, including the Hungarian town of Szombathely.

'**H**istory', says the taxi driver, 'is a nightmare from which we're all of us trying to awake.' He turns to fix me with his blue-eyed stare. 'That's him, that is. James Joyce. Plenty more where that came from, too.' He pauses for effect, and then is off again, at high speed: 'I've got a good one for you:

the British beatitudes – you know what they are? Beef, beer, bulldogs, business, battleships, buggery and bishops.'

I had noticed, on getting into his car, that he had a well-thumbed copy of *Ulysses* wedged alongside the handbrake. When I asked him to take me to Upper Gardiner Street, his face crinkled into a smile. 'That's right in the thick of it,' he declared. 'The Very Reverend John Conmee S. J. of St Francis Xavier's Church stepped on to an outbound tram.' (I gathered he was quoting.) 'The sacred edifice. *The master*. Got it all stored away – for when I'll need it.'

I have already mentioned Joyce, Ireland's favourite literary expatriate. His *Finnegans Wake* is one of the few books that even the most austere scholars are allowed to admit to finding impenetrable. The earlier *Ulysses* is a different matter. It is a plentiful source of half-remembered soundbites among not just Dublin taxi drivers, but also precocious adolescents, flaky émigrés, bar bores (of the erudite, hectoring, whiskey-quaffing variety), international *flâneurs*, crazed Hibernophiles, potty-mouthed booksellers, journalists with English degrees and thieving literary stylists.

Ulysses is 'the book as world' – a cornucopia of experiences and a national epic compressed into a single Dublin day. On 10 June 1904, walking along Nassau Street in Dublin, Joyce saw a tall woman with auburn hair who caught his fancy, and when he spoke with her he found that she worked at a nearby hotel. Six days later they went on what was effectively their first date, a walk at Ringsend. This young woman had a peculiar name, Nora Barnacle, yet as Joyce's biographer Richard Ellmann nicely observes, it could be interpreted as 'an omen of felicitous adhesion'. And so it proved: Joyce's decision to set *Ulysses* on the day he and Nora went for their walk at Ringsend was a tribute typical of the lusty affection she inspired in him.

What happens in Joyce's novel?

Compared with what you'd expect of an airport thriller, not a lot. The two main characters are Stephen Dedalus, a twenty-two-year-old aspiring writer, and Leopold Bloom, an advertising salesman. Stephen is also the main character of Joyce's earlier *A Portrait of the Artist as a Young Man*. Over the course of the day Stephen shares breakfast with his housemates, teaches a couple of classes to unappreciative schoolboys, then loafs about on the beach indulging in a variety of reminiscences, jotting down ideas for poems and picking his nose. At the National Library he has a literary argument with friends, and after some heavy drinking heads into Nighttown, the city's red-light district. 'Life', says Stephen, is 'many days, day after day', and 'we walk through ourselves', meeting a host of other people 'but always meeting ourselves'. A related idea is that society is like a book: immersing yourself in it involves diving deep into your inwardness.

Meanwhile, we see Bloom as he prepares breakfast, which includes a fresh pork kidney, and then as he reads a letter from his daughter and empties his bowels in the outhouse. Heading out, and leaving his wife Molly behind, he picks up another letter at the post office – this time a secret one, from his platonic love Martha Clifford – and goes for a wash at the Turkish baths. Then he attends a funeral, attempts to place an advertisement in the *Freeman's Journal*, has a cheese sandwich and a glass of burgundy for lunch, goes to the Library to look at some statues, dines with Stephen's uncle, is baited by an anti-Semitic 'Citizen', and has an encounter with a young woman on the beach, which culminates in his pleasuring himself. He also worries about the possibility of Molly's infidelity – in fact, she has trysted that very afternoon with Blazes Boylan, the impresario behind a concert she is due to sing at in Belfast – and makes an effort to avert his thoughts on the matter. He visits an acquaintance in hospital, finds Stephen there, and follows the younger man into Nighttown. Bloom defends Stephen after he damages a chandelier in a brothel, and then goes with him to a cab-drivers' shelter for coffee and a bun. They return to Bloom's house for cocoa; they talk, not least about their overlapping lives, and then part. Bloom goes upstairs to Molly, kisses her awake (on the buttocks), and gives her an incomplete account of his day. The book concludes with Molly's silent thoughts as she lies sleepless beside her husband. This final section, which consists of eight very long unpunctuated sentences, is a fantasia of garrulous disappointment and frank sexuality – as well as the inspiration for Kate Bush's song 'The Sensual World'. One early reviewer likened Molly's flow of thoughts to 'a sewer that had burst loose'. My own view is that it is gorgeous.

What exactly makes it so difficult?

The novel's style is famously challenging, and it is meant to be. Among other things, Joyce wanted to evoke the fragmentary nature of thoughts. At the same time he cast the novel as an epic, or as a re-imagining of ancient epic in modern terms: it is modelled not only on the *Odyssey*, but also on Dante's *The Divine Comedy*, and suggests, where Homer celebrated large deeds of heroism, the heroic aspects of ordinary life. According to one reading, Bloom is Odysseus, the wanderer, a.k.a. Ulysses (the Latin form of that name); Stephen is Telemachus, who frets about his country falling into ruin; and Molly is Penelope, besieged by suitors. According to another it is the reader who is Odysseus, journeying in search of meaning. In the novel Joyce tested language, stretching it to see how much bigger a share of life he could convey than other writers had managed to capture. He also tested reading, obliging readers to slow down. You don't have to read *Ulysses* aloud, or hear it read aloud, but both experiences help make sense of it.

One of the difficulties of the novel is that is full of allusions: not just to Homer and Dante, but also to Shakespeare, the Bible, popular songs, Irish politics and innumerable things besides. Joyce is hardly unique in making references to other authors. As is always the case with references of this kind, they can be seen as helping to define the characters and the

---

Five words made up by Joyce – three of them just about self-explanatory

1. smilesmirk
2. Scandiknavery
3. weggebobble (a humorous synonym for *vegetable*)
4. obstropolos (a noisy mouth)
5. pornosophical

---

structure of the book, but they can also be puzzling. I like a friend's complaint, muttered into a very large glass of Czech Pilsner: 'The worst thing is knowing there are allusions, but not knowing what they are or even where they are. How am I supposed to pick up the extra meanings that have been tucked away in the story if I can't even be sure which bits just seem impenetrable and which bits are genuinely meant to be impenetrable?'

At times impenetrably impenetrable, then, Joyce is classified as a modernist – which is to say he is experimental, sensitive to the forces of the Unconscious, difficult, elitist. In *Ulysses* he employs the technique known as stream of consciousness (the term was invented by Henry James's brother, and first used of literature by May Sinclair): the writer transmits the processes of a character's thoughts and emotions. Thus Molly Bloom: 'that lovely fresh plaice I bought I think I'll get a bit of fish tomorrow or today is it Friday yes I will with some blancmange with black currant jam like long ago not those 2 lb pots of mixed plum and apple from the London and Newcastle Williams and Woods goes twice as far only for the bones I hate those eels cod yes I'll get a nice piece of cod I'm always getting enough for 3 forgetting anyway I'm sick of that everlasting butcher's meat.'

Besides passages of interior monologue like this one, *Ulysses* is littered with conversations. It is a relentlessly talky book, a testament to our being a storytelling species. In Joyce, even objects are eloquent: *sllt* goes a machine that sorts the newspapers, a church's bells toll *heighho heighho*, while waves seem to utter the four words *seesoo, hrss, rsseeiss, ooos*. The fire brigade's sirens make a sound like this: *Pflaap!* Animals, such as dogs and a goat, are also articulate. *Mrkrgnao*, cries the Blooms' cat loudly, after an earlier, less agitated *Mkgnao*. (Disappointingly, I have found no record of Joyce owning a cat – or a dog, for that matter. But it's always amused me that one of the wilfully virile Ernest Hemingway's cats was called Thruster.) A hen clucks *Klook*. *Pprrpffrrppffff* goes Bloom's flatulent behind – I defy you to say that out loud and not laugh. Life seems to Bloom a 'parenthesis of infinitesimal brevity'; promiscuity is a way of reaching towards eternity – by leaving behind more traces of oneself – and the novel is above all verbally promiscuous, full of mangled, mishmashed words, like the 'Musemathematics' identified by Bloom as the essence of music.

What marks *Ulysses* out even more, though, is how intensely things are observed and inspected. An obese rat 'toddles'. A bat is 'like a little man in a cloak . . . with tiny hands'. The sky is a 'heaventree of stars hung with humid nightblue fruit'. A firework display kindles the memory of an orgasm: a rocket 'sprang and bang shot blind . . . and it gushed out of it a stream of rain gold hair threads and they shed and ah! they were all greeny dewy stars falling with golden, O so lovely! O, soft, sweet, soft!' Bloom's lunchtime glass of burgundy prompts this: 'Glowing wine on his palate lingered swallowed . . . Seems to a secret touch telling me memory.' The memory it stirs is sexual: kissing a woman once, he took some of the food from her open mouth – 'mawkish pulp her mouth had mumbled sweetsour of her spittle' – and relished the 'young life' of her 'soft warm sticky gumjelly lips'. The humour often results from a similarly close attention to the dreamy absurdity of puns. 'Ham and his descendants mustered and bred there,' thinks Bloom, as he imagines making a sandwich.

Considering the role of the fiction writer, John Updike has wondered, 'Are defecation, tipsy bar babble, days of accumulating small defeats, and tired, compromised, smelly connubial love part of our existence?' Of course they are, he says, and they are all in *Ulysses*. 'I never met a bore,' Joyce claimed; he was at least as attuned to what was interesting in the lives of bank clerks and waiters as to the more obvious matters of interest in the lives of statesmen and soldiers. Perhaps what we really need to say about Joyce is this: he shows that all life is interesting. The grubbier the better, even. Approached by a young man in Zurich who wished to kiss the hand that had written *Ulysses*, Joyce replied that this was not a good idea, for 'it did lots of other things too'.

How to impress when you are on a date with someone bookish

First, a note of caution: should you really be going out, even speculatively, with someone who's overtly literary, if you are not? Now that I've got my squeamishness out of the way, quickly down to business . . .

Joyce's line about his hand – or any variant on it – is off limits. So is anything about 'soft warm sticky gumjelly lips'. This is a good time to be enthusiastic rather than excoriating, but it's not a good time to talk about your love of thirteenth-century religious lyrics. Sound inquisitive, probing, open and adventurous. In the eyes of your beholder, the impression will be this: if you can bring these qualities to bear on books, who knows where else they may present themselves? Try to make comparisons with things you genuinely know about. These should be evaluative. In other words, say 'X is better than Y because X is rhubarb rhubarb'. Except don't say 'better': say 'richer' or 'fresher' or 'denser'. And don't say 'rhubarb'.

5

WOULD YOU REALLY WANT TO JOIN THE DANTE CLUB?

Dante was alive 1265–1321.

His name is pronounced *dan-tay*, with the stress on *dan*. (As with my other recommendations about pronunciation, this suggestion is informed by realism rather than by a pedantic purism.)

Major work: *The Divine Comedy*. Its three parts are the *Inferno*, the *Purgatorio* and the *Paradiso*.

Also wrote: The *Vita Nuova*, and an unfinished philosophical treatise, the *Convivio*.

Trivia: in the preface to the first volume of *Das Kapital* Karl Marx takes as his motto a cheekily amended version of a line in the *Purgatorio*, which he renders as 'Segui il tuo corso, e lascia dir le genti' – 'Go your own way, and let the people talk.' The original, spoken by Virgil to Dante, is 'Vien retro a me, e lascia dir le genti', meaning 'Follow me, and let the people talk'.

For James Joyce, no less important an inspiration than Homer was Dante. From Dante Joyce borrowed characters, images and phrases, and he shared with him the wish to depict an ordinary man's spiritual journey as something beautiful. Joyce sought to be the poet of his people, the Irish, as Dante had been of his. In *Finnegans Wake*, with the conviction that 'I can do anything with words,' Joyce endeavoured to remake his country's language in a cosmopolitan style, as Dante had once forged a new Italian language. The strange dream language of *Finnegans Wake* was never likely to catch on, but there is little doubt that Dante was its inspiration. This Florentine poet's vision has stirred countless imitators and worshippers.

On Coney Island in New York, there used to be an amusement-park ride called Dante's Inferno. It was what is known as a 'dark' ride – a scenic railway passing through unlit caverns, which was punctuated by effigies and grotesques (a devil with his pitchfork, a leering werewolf, a bound man crying for help). What does the ride have to do with Dante Alighieri, an inhabitant of Tuscany in the thirteenth and early fourteenth centuries? Not a great deal, but its title is telling, for Dante's name has become synonymous with the macabre. In popular culture, his works are used to connote a symbolic, spiritually charged air of *noir*, as in the films *Se7en* and *Hannibal* – or in apocalyptic lyrics by Radiohead and the Brazilian heavy metal band Sepultura. In Matthew Pearl's novel *The Dante Club*, set in nineteenth-century Boston, one of the characters comments that Dante writes as Rembrandt paints, 'with a brush dipped in darkness'.

Soldier, diplomat, politician and exile, Dante was a profoundly religious writer, whose works are steeped in his knowledge of the Bible. Much of the Biblical imagery in his writings is invisible to a modern, secular audience. Yet Dante would have summoned it up from memory. 'What's Christianity ever done for the arts?' asks the atheist who chooses to harangue you on an InterCity train. Only try answering the question if you have a lot of time on your hands. You can start by imagining a journey through Italy, from top to toe.

Dante's life was defined by a single love – his love at first sight for the woman he would call Beatrice, Bice di Folco Portinari. Dante, it seems, met Beatrice when he was nine and she was eight. In their late teens they got to know each other properly. But Beatrice married another man, Simone dei Bardi, in 1287 and died of plague three years later at the age of twenty-four. Distraught, Dante sought consolation in studying philosophy and in writing his first book, the *Vita Nuova*, a mixture of poems and prose in which he hymns Beatrice, without commenting on the fact of her death, and tries to embrace the possibility of a brighter future – rather than wallowing in the belief that Beatrice's death is a symptom of mankind's damnation. The *Vita Nuova* engages with a question that consumed Dante's contemporaries: 'What is love?' It is a question that preoccupies us still – the subject of countless poems and songs, philosophical investigations, spiritualist noodlings, magazine articles, psychiatric studies, sermons and films. Plenty of times I've argued with friends over whether there is any word more often cheapened, abused, exaggerated, deified. Dante says that love is 'an accident in substance'; it does not exist in itself, but only as a property of a substance – that is, a person who is capable of loving. For Dante, love is a collusion between the body, the mind and the senses.

What is Dante's great achievement?

The *Vita Nuova* is extraordinary in the way it glorifies a human being – extraordinary, that is, because in the thirteenth century such glorification was expected to be reserved for God. But Dante's reputation rests on the work we call *The Divine Comedy*, a stunning vision of the hereafter. The adjective 'divine' was attached to it by his first biographer, Giovanni Boccaccio, and only came to be permanently associated with it several hundred years after his death. To its author this three-part poem – comprising the *Inferno*, the *Purgatorio* and the *Paradiso* – was simply the *Commedia*. As for its being a 'comedy', this is partly because of an old definition that classifies as 'comic' whatever is written in a plain, realistic style; Dante wrote *The Divine Comedy* in his own Tuscan dialect, rather than in Latin. But in any case the basic movement of the work is from suffering towards happiness (from the inferno to paradise) and this trajectory – towards redemption – makes it possible to think of the poem, taken as a whole, as having the potential to please and delight, as a more orthodox comedy would.

It has become a sort of academic cliché to compare this triple-decker masterpiece to a Gothic cathedral: a confident and structurally impressive assertion of Christianity, immersed in the colour of the Middle Ages. (A pedant might argue that it is less Gothic than Romanesque.) Each of its three 'canticles' comprises thirty-three cantos or sections; there is also a preliminary canto, so the total number is a round hundred. Its verses, each of three lines, interlock; the second line of every verse rhymes with the first and third lines of the one that follows. This form, called *terza rima*, has been seen by some as a representation of the Holy Trinity, and by others as resembling the helical structure of DNA. The verses are always pushing forward, yet always overlapping: the reader feels the continuous movement of the poem, and does so expectantly, waiting for its echoes. The poem's force is cumulative. Nevertheless, plenty of people have tried to home in on the best bits of *The Divine Comedy*. The poet Shelley sought out 'those fortunate isles laden with golden fruit' – the gorgeously quotable passages – and maintained that these 'alone could tempt anyone to embark in the misty ocean of his dark and extravagant fiction'. Here Shelley seems a bit like the person at your birthday party who chips the icing off your cake.

Dante's poetry has given rise to a massive amount of commentary. Yet for all the explanatory notes and insights that cluster around it, the experience of the poem is straightforwardly exciting. Take, for example, the very opening: the lines 'Nel mezzo del cammin di nostra vita / mi ritrovai per una selva oscura, / ché la diritta via era smarrita' ('In the middle of our journey in life, I found myself in a dark wood, as the correct route had become unclear'). The narrator is looking back to a time when he was unsure of himself. We are to understand that he was halfway to reaching his allotted 'threescore years and ten' – he was thirty-five – and could be said to have been in the throes of a midlife crisis. Readers will recognize what he was going through, whether or not we have reached that stage in life. The 'selva oscura' is the darkness of depression or of the more macabre side of our imagination. And in speaking of 'nostra vita' Dante indicates that his experience, while personal, is also universal.

What is Dante's appeal?

The journey, the dark wood, the uncertainty of identifying the correct route: here, right away, is the nub of Dante's interest for a modern audience. We all know about being lost. Lost in the chaos of everyday life, lost spiritually and emotionally, lost on the way to that little seafood restaurant we keep hearing about but no one seems to be able to point out on a map. Most of us also know about being found, about finding ourselves. The dark wood is a place inside us. 'How am I feeling? I'm having a bit of a Dante moment. You know, plumbing the depths.' Somehow when I think of *The Divine Comedy* I can't help feeling that it needs to be read with a glass of strong liquor to hand. The journey 'upward' – to enlightenment – is first a journey down, into the shadows.

The deeper readers go into *The Divine Comedy*, the more it equips them with what seem to be helpful points of reference. The idea of voyaging into the world beyond this one is much older than Dante, but feels vital to a modern audience. What happens when you die? And what happens, for that matter, while you are alive and you descend into the subterranean reaches of your psyche?

The first part, the *Inferno*, pictures Dante's descent into hell, which is presented as a city made by God as a kind of punishment centre. Dante is a sinner, mired in doubt. His guide is Virgil, who explains among other things that in this place the human mind, such a magnificent instrument, has shrivelled into uselessness. The task is Virgil's because he embodies a mix of aesthetic sensitivity, reason and knowledge, yet also because he was believed to have prophesied in the

Eclogues the birth of Christ. He has been sent by Beatrice to help Dante on his way.

One of the achievements of *The Divine Comedy* is a sense of what it really means to go on a journey. Dante is a tourist, and tourism is a way of discovering the breadth and depth of humankind. Early on, images of sin encroach from every side. Every kind of sin, too. At the outset he is shown three kinds: self-indulgence, violence and fraud. Others follow. As Dante proceeds, anonymous crowds move restlessly. All these people were once living, and all have chosen their situations in their afterlife: the way they lived is directly answered by their punishments in hell. Dante's path is often barred, but his guide persuades the impeding figures to step aside, for Dante must see everything: he has been sent to sample all the flavours of experience. One of the qualities of Dante's journey is that he pays attention to all the things he sees, and he seems to pay each of them just the right amount of attention.

We speak of being 'in hell', of something being 'a living hell' – moving house, working for an unpleasant employer, depression, extracting oneself from a damaged relationship. What does hell look like? Dante thinks of it as a funnel, sucking you in. It is from Dante that we get the idea of the circles of hell – 'Listening to this Westlife song is worse than being in the ninth circle of hell.' As Dante travels down from the first circle toward the ninth and last, he encounters increasingly wicked people. In each circle people are punished in a way appropriate to their crimes. This is a slickly organized place, a bit like a nightmare office, with a retained staff of functionaries and enforcers dispensing justice in an utterly inflexible fashion.

The nine circles of hell in Dante's *Inferno*

First circle: otherwise known as Limbo, this is the residence of people who have not been baptized and of pagans who have managed to live virtuously.

Second circle: the people here are guilty of lustfulness and sensual living. The word for 'lust' is *talento*, which combines talent, pleasure, desire, wilfulness and impulsiveness. This circle's residents are buffeted by winds that recall the stormy forces of lust.

Third circle: home of the gluttons, people who have behaved like pigs. They lie in a slush that reminds them of the junk they ate during their lives.

Fourth circle: this is where Dante finds those who have been guilty of an excessive concern with material goods – squandering them or stashing them away. Those guilty of avarice push heavy weights in one direction, while those guilty of wastefulness push them in the opposite direction.

Fifth circle: the angry zone, where people who have been wrathful or sullen reside. The wrathful fight, while the others lie gurgling underwater.

Sixth circle: here are the heretics, whose burning iron tombs are symbols of their obstinacy in denying God.

Seventh circle: the violent zone, comprising people who have been physically violent (they are steeped in a boiling river of blood), suicides (torn at by harpies), and those guilty of blasphemy, sodomy or usury (who lie on hot sand, beneath a shower of flakes of fire).

Eighth circle: this circle contains a variety of people who consciously did evil, including flatterers (who are steeped in faeces), corrupt politicians (who are supervised by devils), thieves (who are bitten by snakes), and hypocrites (who wear cloaks that appear to be made of gold but are actually made of lead).

Ninth circle: here are the traitors, trapped in an icy lake. Among their number are Judas Iscariot and Satan. Judas is being skinned alive, while Satan cries unceasingly.

Dante's image of hell was drawn, of course, from the world. He is among the dead, but he speaks of the living. Hell is to a large degree modelled on Dante's own Florence, a 'terra prava' (depraved homeland), the scene of crime, greed and malign politics. Often a particular character from the past comes into focus, such as Filippo Argenti, a notoriously repellent member of the Adimari family, who earned the nickname Argenti after having his horse shod with silver. Here he rises out of his bed of slime and accosts Dante. He's then set upon by the mob, who are determined, like football hooligans, to 'get' this showy symbol of 'the other side'. There are several explanations for Dante's decision to pick out Filippo Argenti in this way: he may have plundered Dante's possessions after the poet was forced to leave Florence, blocked his readmission to the city, or simply smacked him round the head. Whatever the truth, his name survives for all the wrong reasons, and among the questions Dante raises is this: is it acceptable to use literature to achieve revenge? Another concern Dante raises, as he shows us that hell contains likeable characters as well as loathsome ones, is how we feel about the fates of those we love who have strayed from the path of right.

Readers sometimes get stuck in the gloom of the *Inferno*, and as a result think Dante is a morbid sort, obsessed with torture. Its most famous lines – and thus Dante's most famous lines – are usually translated as 'Abandon hope, all ye who enter here.' But this is not the message of *The Divine Comedy* as a whole, and the *Inferno* is really a prologue to what follows.

Thus the *Purgatorio* is not just a sequel to the *Inferno*; it is a resurrection. This middle section of Dante's work explores the question of how personal freedom can be reconciled with the demands of a Christian faith. It presents extraordinary and often baffling landscapes, much less familiar to the medieval imagination than depictions of heaven and hell were. To a modern audience, the word 'purgatory' brings to mind wholly negative images. Not so for Dante and his contemporaries. Dante's purgatory is the place between hell and paradise, a mountain where 'l'umano spirito si purga / e di salire al ciel diventa degno' – that is, where the human spirit purifies itself and becomes worthy to ascend into heaven. The people in purgatory have done wrong, but in the end they have turned to God. They are redeemed by love and will end up in paradise.

Mount Purgatory is a hard place, but the mood is different from in the *Inferno*. Its inhabitants, unlike Filippo Argenti and his kind, are casting off their earthly characteristics, and instead of being sharply defined as individuals they are joined together in groups. Penance is collaborative. The upward journey, which occupies three days and nights, takes in seven terraces – one for each of the Seven Deadly Sins – and at the summit is the

Garden of Eden, sensuously described. There Dante is reunited with Beatrice. The moment she appears, Virgil vanishes (as a pagan, he cannot enter paradise), and Dante is shocked to tears by his going. When Beatrice then speaks, her first word is his name – the only time it appears in the whole of *The Divine Comedy*. The moment of reunion is a focal point in the entire work. We might expect a conventional tear-jerking embrace; instead Beatrice scolds Dante, reminding him of his responsibilities to his Creator, pointing out that he has erred, and insisting he pay the tax of penitence, which is crucial to his spiritual renewal. Dante confesses his shortcomings, is baptized afresh in the River Eunoë (literally 'Good mind' or 'Good remembrance'), and is able at the end of the *Purgatorio* to continue, regenerated, towards the stars.

In the *Paradiso*, Dante journeys through the visible heavens to the invisible place known as the Empyrean. Initially he is guided by Beatrice, and love replaces hopefulness as the keynote, but on reaching the Empyrean he must bid her farewell in order to behold the majesty of the Holy Trinity. Now God's glory is shown shining through the whole of Creation and giving it order. The focus shifts from Dante the man to Dante the poet. In the first two parts of *The Divine Comedy* the poet is safe and the pilgrim in danger: now the positions are reversed. Dante repeatedly claims that language cannot do justice to the fullness of experience. He says, for instance, that he cannot express even a thousandth of the truth of Beatrice's smile. This seems to be modesty on his part, but, in practice, Dante goes where other poets had not dared to go – into the realm of the imagination, the misty subjectivity of the mind, the land of pure metaphor. And that is our next port of call.

6

DO YOU NEED TO BOTHER
WITH POETRY?

Poetry is sometimes described as one of the enlargements of
life. Dante is one of those who most powerfully demonstrate
this: he makes universal truths individual, shapes the contours of
the imagination, and transforms the raw materials of history into
things of beauty. Yet poetry attracts hostility and, more often,
blithe dismissal. 'I don't like poetry,' otherwise sophisticated
people say – or, in the unapologetically apologetic version, 'I'm
sorry, but I really don't like poetry.' Alternatively, they reflect, as
of modern jazz, 'I like it in principle, but just never get it.' Bound
up with this, commonly, is the belief that poetry is useless. 'Poetry
makes nothing happen,' as W. H. Auden, himself a poet, wrote.

Is this really the case? Auden's line takes on different reso-
nances according to where you lay the stress. Try putting it on
'poetry', then on 'nothing', and then on 'happen'. In doing so,
you're reading the line as a poet would wish. I suspect Auden's
point is that poetry cannot make anything happen in the material world, but there are other areas in which it *can* make things
happen.

Already I have suggested that poetry activates the mind and
makes full use of the resources of language. It externalizes

feelings that might not otherwise be voiced. It may even achieve some of the ritual effects of religion. Poets have often been spokespeople, and I don't think it's too hopeful to say that they can be historians, entertainers, magicians, therapists and educators as well as propagandists and rabble-rousers.

Do you really have to *talk* about it?

Conversations about poetry tend to happen only with poets. And how often, unless you are a poet yourself, do you interact with them? There are three things to know about poets. They are all obsessed with epiphanies – those moments of sharp realization when a person makes sense of his or her relationship with the past, a place or another individual. They're all damaged, and their work is where they repair the damage. Plus, to steal an old joke, you should never trust a poet who can drive.

But there is a kind of conversation about poetry that does happen more often: a conversation with yourself. A little piece of poetry can be made to last a long time. I remember noticing this as a teenager; a line could be savoured, turned around and re-examined in the same way that a boiled sweet could be kept in the mouth, exuding flavour, for far longer than it seemed reasonable to imagine. Bite off a chunk of a poem, and you could make it last all day. The last lines of Tennyson's 'Ulysses' – which is based not on Homer, but on an episode in Dante's *Inferno* – are as follows:

> That which we are, we are;
> One equal temper of heroic hearts,

> Made weak by time and fate, but strong in will
> To strive, to seek, to find, and not to yield.

That last line sounds totally confident. However, Christopher Ricks, one of the best modern analysts of poetry, comments that 'rippling underneath that final line, striving to utter itself but battened down by will, is another line, almost identical and yet utterly different: "To strive, to seek, to yield, and not to find".' This insight may not convince everyone, but it suggests the way a line of poetry can contain two forces: its rhythm, and an undertow that pulls it in the opposite direction. The undertow is one of the things that make poetry complicatedly satisfying.

What readers most enjoy about poetry, though, are its sounds and textures, the rustle of language. The succulence of poetic diction is not just pleasurable, but powerful. T. S. Eliot wrote that poetry can communicate before it is understood, and the truth of this is evident in Eliot's own works. Scholarly, mystical and adept at putting on strange voices, Eliot often leaves the reader perplexed, but his most difficult lines are also very quotable.

To take a rather more extreme example: my German, while not non-existent, leaves much to be desired, yet I can still savour a line by Rainer Maria Rilke ('Befiehl den letzten Früchten voll zu sein') or Bertolt Brecht ('Sieh den Nagel in der Wand, den du eingeschlagen hast'). In translation, these lines are less toothsome: 'Bid the last fruits to be full' and 'Behold the nail in the wall, the one you have driven in.' Brecht, incidentally, is best known as a playwright and a theorist of drama, but in Germany his poetry is held in high regard.

A further incidental, which I can't resist including: in Irvine Welsh's *Trainspotting*, the main character, Mark Renton, impresses some women on a train by talking about Brecht. I'll drink to that.

How can poetry affect its readers?

One of the things poetry enables is a reframing of experience, a closer knowing of what we think we already know. It teaches the reader to see better. (James Joyce can be thought of as a poet.) The Victorian poet Gerard Manley Hopkins adopted, from the medieval philosopher John Duns Scotus, the notion of *haecceitas* – literally, 'thisness' – to suggest the intense individuality of an object. Looking at a flower, for instance, Hopkins was acutely aware that it was *this* flower rather than some other flower. Hopkins's poems are full of moments where he looks deep into this particularity. What he sees are the 'silk-sack' clouds, the 'bright boroughs' of the starlit sky, the 'liquid waist' of a working ploughman.

By the same token, a modest stash of poetry can fund a good deal of wise-sounding chat. I have a friend who, to my knowledge, has only ever read one poem, but he manages to reference it at every available opportunity. The poem is not a short one (T. S. Eliot's *The Waste Land*), and he has read it several times, but the investment has paid handsome dividends. If someone were to recite the whole of *The Waste Land* while we walked together through the City of London, I might be impressed by his powers of retention, but it is more likely, I suspect, that I would think he was a bit odd. However, someone who quotes a tiny sliver of *The Waste Land* – knowingly, but without ostentation – may actually pass for being quite cool. My friend, whom I'll call Adam, can slip into Eliot's lingo rather the way an aficionado of Monty Python can trot out the Dead Parrot sketch. You sneeze while playing poker: 'Madame Sosostris, famous clairvoyante, / Had a bad cold, nevertheless / Is known to be the wisest woman in Europe, / With a wicked pack of cards.' Somebody's been jilted: 'When lovely woman stoops to folly and / Paces about her room again, alone, / She smoothes her hair with automatic hand, / And puts a record on the gramophone.' The poem has become, for Adam, a sort of panacea.

Reading poetry can resemble homeopathy. By consuming a tiny dose of something, we may be able to protect ourselves against its undiluted form. 'Like cures like,' essentially. (The practice is more credible in the case of the poetry than it is in the realm of medicine.) The idea is an old one. George Puttenham, in an essay published more than 400 years ago, spoke of the poet as a 'physician'. 'It is a piece of joy to be able to lament with ease': when one is sad, 'the very grief itself' may contribute to the 'cure of the disease'. If you're ever stuck in an uncomfortable conversation about a poet, a foolproof way of knocking the conversation dead is to say 'He helped me a lot when I was in a bad place.' If you are talking to someone who isn't English, he or she will want to hear about this bad place – a great opportunity to discuss something you really know about, namely yourself. And if you are talking to someone English, especially the male variety, absolute revulsion at the prospect of speaking about feelings will move the conversation into some much less torrid zone.

The critic Harold Bloom proposes poetry as 'the crown of imaginative literature', because it 'does us a kind of violence . . . to startle us out of our sleep-of-death into a more capacious sense of life'. Poems not only make us see familiar things afresh, but also make the alien seem pleasingly approachable. When Robert Burns pronounces that his love – both the feeling of being in love and the person he loves – is 'like a red, red rose / That's newly sprung in June', we understand the vitality of his emotions, their freshness and the freshness of their object. John Milton describes the tumultuous occasion of Satan being cast out of heaven, and writes that God hurled him 'headlong flaming from th'ethereal sky / With hideous ruin and combustion down / To bottomless perdition, there to dwell / In adamantine chains and penal fire'. The lines chart Satan's descent – flaming down to dwell in fire. Say them. Can't you hear him falling? The key thing here is, I think, that it is pretty much impossible not to pause between 'combustion' and 'down', so that the word 'down', detached from its own line, hurries the reader into the next line, enacting the sheer downwardness of Satan's fall.

An enthusiastic school English teacher, making this point to a class of sixth-formers, might well notice a few raised eyebrows. 'Miss, don't you think you're just over-analysing? This Milton, yeah – he may have been clever, but you can't seriously say he meant us to think *that*.' We might step into the shoes of the teacher at this point (brown court shoes, size 6) and invent a suitable riposte. Here's one: 'The effect of the text isn't *in* the text, waiting for us to recover it. Instead, it's in us, the audience.' Alternatively: 'If you can see it, it's there to be seen.' For instance, in *The Borderers*, his attempt at a tragedy after the model of Shakespeare, William Wordsworth writes:

> Action is transitory – a step, a blow,
> The motion of a muscle – this way or that –
> 'Tis done, and in the after-vacancy
> We wonder at ourselves like men betrayed:
> Suffering is permanent, obscure and dark,
> And shares the nature of infinity.

To me this sounds modern. *'Tis* doesn't, of course, but the rest does. Notice especially how 'after-vacancy' hangs at the end of the line, not followed by any punctuation: reading this, saying it especially, we hear the space, the 'vacancy' that follows the kind of action Wordsworth imagines, and we occupy that space with the wonder Wordsworth describes. In passing, I think I ought to add that this tragedy of Wordsworth's is the kind of thing it's good to know about, because people usually think of him as being 'only' a poet. It's handy to know some titbits about authors' lesser works – what Tolstoy and Joyce and Austen got up to when they weren't busy with the books on which their reputations now rest.

While philosophers refresh the language of political and moral thought, poets most importantly refresh the language of the emotions. This is easy to say, but needs to be shown. First, a few short examples. In his long poem *The Princess*, Tennyson writes of 'the dark dissolving human heart'. My first reaction is to wonder if the heart is dissolving something, or if it is being dissolved; the ambiguity is pregnant. And is it dark because its contents are secret or because – not the same thing – it contains some sinister secret? Even completely removed from their context, these words are intriguing as a generalization about the human heart. Tennyson is fluent in this emotional music. In

A fistful of poetic openings that everybody knows (I say this with an eyebrow slightly raised)

1. 'Of Man's first disobedience, and the fruit / Of that forbidden tree, whose mortal taste / Brought death into the world, and all our woe, / With loss of Eden . . . / Sing, heavenly Muse' (John Milton, *Paradise Lost*)
2. 'And did those feet in ancient time / Walk upon England's mountains green?' (William Blake, preface to his epic poem *Milton*)
3. 'April is the cruellest month' (T. S. Eliot, *The Waste Land*)
4. 'I met a traveller from an antique land . . .' (Percy Bysshe Shelley, 'Ozymandias')
5. 'Ethereal minstrel! Pilgrim of the sky! / Dost thou despise the earth where cares abound?' (William Wordsworth, 'To a Skylark')
6. 'How do I love thee? Let me count the ways' (Elizabeth Barrett Browning, *Sonnets from the Portuguese*, 43)
7. 'My heart aches, and a drowsy numbness pains / My sense, as though of hemlock I had drunk' (John Keats, 'Ode to a Nightingale')

another of his long poems, *In Memoriam*, he returns to the house of his dead friend Arthur Henry Hallam, and is faced with 'Doors, where my heart was used to beat / So quickly, waiting for a hand'. Take out 'was', and this is the language of everyday speech. But this is not to say that it lacks craft. Notice how the line speeds up after the first comma, just as Tennyson's heart used to race at the thought of seeing his friend. The ghost of Hallam's touch haunts him; the unspecific 'a hand' seems particularly forlorn. Moreover, 'beat' rhymes with the last word of the line before it, 'Here in the long unlovely street', which creates a slight interruption before the intensity of 'So quickly'. This has the effect of making the reader acknowledge just what it feels like to have a quickly beating heart.

A different sort of example is Robert Lowell's line 'The Lord survives the rainbow of His will.' Here the rainbow, traditionally understood as a symbol of divine promise, seems less certain – even deathly. 'Survives' is the key word. In common with much of the best writing, the whole line and this choice of verb in particular prompt the reaction 'This is strange.' Meaning is being withheld. This holding back of information can be achieved through the order of words as well as through the selection of vocabulary. Thus, praising his lover, John Donne writes, 'She is all states, and all princes I, / Nothing else is.' The words 'Nothing else is' feel delayed, rather stagily – and this is the true shape of a lover's hyperbole, building to an extravagant oversimplification. As for the sun that beams through the window, 'since thy duties be / To warm the world, that's done in warming us. / Shine here to us, and thou art everywhere; / This bed thy centre is, these walls thy sphere.' The sun's rays slant in through the curtains, lighting up the bedroom, the bed. 'Nothing else is': right now, the poet is the hub of the solar system. Furthermore, while Donne is in charge ('all princes'), without the woman (who is 'all states') he would have nothing to be in charge *of*. The image, which at first glance suggests an arrogant attitude on Donne's part, on closer consideration reveals how he depends on his lover – and at the same time reveals, more subtly, how the absolute power of monarchs is itself a rhetorical and theatrical performance.

Five poetic forms

Ode. Conventionally, an ode is a meditative and dignified poem, which addresses its subject directly. Examples are John Keats's 'Ode on Melancholy' and, in an admittedly less serious vein, Adam Sandler's 'Ode to My Car'.

Elegy. A sombre poem concerned with mourning, often following a person's death. Celebrated examples in English are Thomas Gray's 'Elegy Written in a Country Churchyard' and John Milton's 'Lycidas' (in memory of his university friend Edward King, who drowned in the Irish Sea).

Sonnet. Literally a 'little song', this is a poem of fourteen lines, often concerned with love, and usually divided into two sections of eight lines and six (known as the octave and the sestet). The octave may propose some sort of question, which the sestet then resolves. The most celebrated early 'sonneteer' was the fourteenth-century Italian known as Petrarch. In English the form, most often associated with Shakespeare, was pioneered by Sir Thomas Wyatt in the 1520s.

Haiku. This form, which originated in Japan, consists of a mere seventeen syllables, and often takes as its subject nature or man's place in the natural world. The first and last of its three lines contains five syllables: the middle line contains seven. The master of the form is generally reckoned to be the seventeenth-century poet Matsuo Bashō.

Ballad. Usually a ballad is a story told in the form of a song, consisting of short lines. Ballads make heavy use of rhyme and often contain a chorus. A classic example is the traditional song 'Scarborough Fair'; a more modern one is Don McLean's 'American Pie'.

How do poems convey their 'truth'?

The Marxist critic Terry Eagleton suggests that of all the forms of literature poetry is the one 'most sequestered from the winds of history'. (By 'sequestered' he means, I think, 'secluded'.) It is 'language which is about itself', where 'the relationship between word and meaning . . . is tighter than it is in everyday speech', and 'the meaning of its words is closely bound up with the experience of them'. Furthermore, it bridges the divide between rational thought and what he calls 'a number of enticing but dangerous forms of irrationalism'. Its 'devotion to meaning' is pursued in a way that permits 'the rhythms, images and impulses of our subterranean life to speak through its crisp exactitudes'.

I like the sound of 'crisp exactitudes', but some of the time what gives pleasure to readers of poetry is blurry. Distinctness is something that poets may try to achieve, but the failure to achieve it can be just as powerful. For instance, Philip Larkin, who is no favourite of Eagleton's, begins a poem, 'The trees are coming into leaf / Like something almost being said' – and among the responses this draws is the question 'What is it that might almost be said?' The word which isn't said, but which we are likely to expect is 'again': 'The trees are coming into leaf *again*.' There is promise here, but also a hint of a stammer, a hesitation. Is something wrong? Are the coming leaves in some way sad? Actually, the simile can be seen as inexact, because the 'something almost being said' may in the end be said, but may remain unsaid, whereas the trees *will* get their leaves. Nevertheless, the line feels true. The eloquence of a moment can come, as Larkin hints, from a place behind or underneath the words. This perception is not exactly crisp or exact, yet it does convey a truth about the 'subterranean' part of life.

Here, finally, is the Argentine poet Leopoldo Lugones: 'Iba el silencio andando como un largo lebrel' ('Silence was moving like a long greyhound'). Why a long greyhound? Why a greyhound at all? Does silence actually move? Can it? I have removed the line from its context, but this is what happens to lines of poetry – they are appropriated. Does it help to know that Lugones killed himself with cyanide while on holiday, or that over the course of his literary career he gravitated from socialism to fascism? Maybe it does, but you don't *need* to know these things, because the line is interesting enough to survive in isolation. I can puzzle over it for some time. How does its sound contribute to its effect?

Here, as with any line of poetry, one of the games you can play is to see how much its mood and meaning can be altered by changing a single word. Imagine revising one word in each of the seven examples in the box on page 89. 'How do I love thee? Let me state the ways.' 'I met a traveller from a distant land.' 'My heart aches, and a dozy numbness pains / My sense.' So much is lost through this kind of variation, and changing or removing just one word undermines the poem's architecture, the shape that organizes its purposes, the sense of its truth.

What to do if someone wants to talk to you about Milton

I've mentioned John Milton and his masterpiece *Paradise Lost* – a major literary figure and a major work, but hardly the stuff of coffee-shop banter. Anyone who chooses to engage you on the subject of Milton, outside the context of a university interview, is likely to be an autodidact – by which I mean self-taught, to a fearsome degree. In the eyes of auto-didacts, John Milton is the Godfather of political radicalism, revolutionary poetry and personal liberty; they consider a close knowledge of *Paradise Lost* to be one of the true marks of a serious mind. The philosopher Georg Hegel is another figure lionized by the self-taught. What steps should you take if someone confronts you with the ghosts of Milton or Hegel? In the words of one of my more passionately self-educated friends, 'Run like hell. Consider buying a gun.'

7

SHAKESPEARE: MUCH ADO ABOUT NOTHING?

Shakespeare was born in 1564 and died in 1616.

Major works: thirty-seven plays (the number is not set in stone, as his authorship of several works is disputed) and a sequence of 154 sonnets. Most of the plays are famous, with the best known including *Hamlet*, *Othello*, *Macbeth*, *Romeo and Juliet*, *King Lear*, *The Merchant of Venice*, historical plays such as *Henry V*, and 'Roman' ones such as *Julius Caesar*.

Also wrote: two long narrative poems, *Venus and Adonis* and *The Rape of Lucrece*.

Trivia: all bar one of the twenty-seven moons of the planet Uranus are named after characters in Shakespeare. The exception is Umbriel, which takes its name from a character in Alexander Pope's poem *The Rape of the Lock*.

In the classic British film *Withnail and I*, Uncle Monty, a failed actor, reflects that 'It is the most shattering experience in a young man's life when he wakes up one morning and quite reasonably says to himself, "I shall never play the Dane."' Many of the film's predominantly male fans understand this instinctively: 'the Dane', Hamlet, is in all of us, they feel, and each man is at some time inclined to suspect that his interpretation of the role would be special, both as an expression of his own humanity (that is, special for him) and as a reading of the play (that is, special for its audience). But plenty of people could not care less about Hamlet. He is just a name. His vast inner world of self is no more knowable than the Pinwheel Galaxy. And for every person enraptured by Shakespeare's art, there has been a sceptic just as deeply convinced of his lack of worth. King George III laughingly complained to the novelist Fanny Burney, who was 'second keeper' of his wife Queen Charlotte's robes, 'Was there ever such stuff as . . . Shakespeare?' By 'stuff' he meant bad stuff, and he went into considerable detail about it, before concluding that of course 'nobody dare abuse' the national treasure and 'one should be stoned for saying so!'

King George was unusually candid, but it was easy for him. For the majority, Shakespeare is intimidating. He is *the* English author, a monarch among writers, extravagantly revered and at the same time feared and loathed. In short, an icon. This almost certainly has something to do with the circumstances in which most people first come across his works: in school. Some cruel educational philosophy dictates that many children must study one of the Bard's more stultifying plays (*Measure for Measure*, in my case) and must pay especially close attention to the scenes of comic relief, which typically involve unamusing puns about codpieces and leaky vessels and dollars (or should that be dolours? *Ho-ho*). If they are especially privileged, they are taken to see a bad production of the play they have been studying, probably put on by crackheads at the local leisure centre. Once installed in their cramped seats, they fantasize about the interval – a chance to buy some Maltesers, or, better still, an illicit bottle of beer – and furtively attempt to listen to their iPods. Audacious teachers (or possibly just lazy ones) show their classes the DVD of Baz Luhrmann's brashly saturnalian take on *Romeo and Juliet*, and pay the penalty of hearing their students complain, 'I liked it, apart from the language.'

The language is what makes Shakespeare. Paraphrase kills the drama and the characters. 'Light thickens, / And the crow makes wing to th'rooky wood.' 'Death lies on her like an untimely frost / Upon the sweetest flower of all the field.' But it's fair to say that studying this language is probably not the best route into the plays for the uninitiated. Some of it has become proverbial – 'parting is such sweet sorrow', 'all the world's a stage', 'the ripest fruit first falls' – but the bits that have not attained soundbite status can seem impenetrable. And it's all weighed down with so much baggage. Shakespeare's contemporaries would have found some of it difficult, too; they would have been puzzled by the words he imported from other languages and by the new terms he coined. The complexity of his wordplay – in the wilful ambiguities and brisk comic exchanges – remains unsettling. But modern audiences tend to be troubled, most fundamentally, by his vocabulary and syntax.

What does Shakespeare have to say to an audience today?

There are references in the plays that are evidently topical, and the dramas relate to this historical context in ways that are no longer readily apparent. How much do we need to know about Queen Elizabeth's hostility to the increasing numbers of 'black-moors' in London before we can grapple with *Othello*? How important is it that *Macbeth* was written partly to flatter the new king, James I, who was a Scot with a keen interest in witch-craft? Or that Shakespeare was on at least one occasion a money-lender, like Shylock in *The Merchant of Venice*, and that he was an actor, known for his performance as the Ghost in *Hamlet*? If we miss these contexts, if we are unaware of them, hasn't something been lost? The classic refrain among Shakespeare-haters is that his works are no longer relevant. They're all about kings and queens, aren't they, or full of stuffy dukes and incompre-hensible clowns?

Well, *no*. Families are torn apart by jealousy, lovers' vows and virtue are tested, and parents suffocate their children. Desperation leads to suicide, sexual inadequacies cripple reason, racist hatred festers, the lust for power and money overwhelms decency and truth, members of viciously opposed clans fall in love, and politics seethes with corruption, while the folly and pity of war are mercilessly exposed. Is this alien, irrelevant? Characters make poignantly inappropriate jokes, like Mercutio in *Romeo and Juliet*, who says of the wound that will kill him, 'No, 'tis not so deep as a well, nor so wide as a / Church door; but 'tis enough, 'twill serve.' The audience, when it laughs, does so with a full consciousness of the anxiety that informs its laughter. Shakespeare invents a new type of comedy which involves laughing with its characters, rather than at them. When Hamlet speaks of 'the law's delay' and 'the insolence of office' we are likely to recognize the tortuous prevarications of legal experts and the offensive contemptuousness of administrators and bureaucrats, the jobsworth's impatient discourtesy. Sex, conflict, materialism, the inadequacies of religion, the dependence of high society on servants and functionaries: all are here, realistically portrayed.

Not many people *read* Shakespeare's plays – that's reckoned dull fare, the stuff of the classroom – and of his other works only the sonnets are much perused. (Of these, more in a moment.) But Shakespeare is all around us. His afterlives are myriad. He has become a staple of popular culture. His characters pop up in songs by Bob Dylan and Bruce Springsteen, and he is referenced by Captain Kirk in *Star Trek*, as well as in porn films, comic books, theme parks and *The Muppet Show*.

Anthony Burgess, author of *A Clockwork Orange*, was once assured by a schoolmate that Shakespeare could be fun: 'It's all fighting and fucking whores!' Thankfully, Shakespeare occasionally rises above the hyperactive chutzpah of a Guy Ritchie movie. There is a lot of fighting – be it the tense tussle between Macbeth and his nemesis Macduff, or the mass carnage of *Titus Andronicus*, in which ten murders happen on stage – and there are a few bits about 'fucking whores', but there is plenty besides.

For instance, there is the pathos of King Lear, holding in his arms the corpse of his favourite daughter Cordelia, saying 'She's dead as earth,' but then wishfully thinking the opposite – 'Lend me a looking-glass; / If that her breath will mist or stain the stone, / Why then she lives.' Or, in *The Winter's Tale*, of Leontes gazing at a statue of his wife Hermione, whom he has long thought dead, and experiencing a sudden dart of passionate realization: 'O, she's warm.' Or even of Cressida, forced to part in the morning from her lover Troilus, simply stating, 'Night hath been too brief.' And there is a different kind of deep charge – pathetic, yes, but comic too – when Falstaff, the 'huge hill of flesh' who is the companion of Prince Hal in the two parts of *Henry IV*, claims he has been attacked by 'three . . . knaves in Kendal green'. For when the attack happened it was pitch dark – so dark that Falstaff couldn't even have seen his own hand, as Hal points out. The Kendal-green clothes of his assailants are a risible fabrication. Just the sort of thing we expect from a bad liar who is trying desperately hard to be a good one. Falstaff, incidentally, is described in some marvellously unpleasant ways: as a 'horse-breaker', 'fat-kidneyed rascal', 'gross fat man', 'claybrained guts', 'bed-presser', 'oily rascal' and 'whoreson obscene greasy tallow-keech'. W. H. Auden made the disconcerting claim that 'If Falstaff were running the world, it would be like the Balkans.'

Shakespeare shows us the essence of human nature by drawing attention to those little details that are the trophies of a rich existence. Many people will recognize the heartening experience of reading or hearing about a fictional character's anxieties and thinking 'So it's not just me!' In Shakespeare these moments of recognition are legion, and there are also countless moments when we see something as we have seen it a hundred or a thousand times before – but this time with a special sharpness that pierces through all the dreariness of life and makes us smile or frown or nod or wince. When we see them, then, we

recognize the schoolboy 'with his satchel / And shining morning face, creeping like snail / Unwillingly to school' and the
lick-spittling lackey 'doting on his own obsequious bondage',
and we recognize the way a person who depends on an unreliable ally 'swims with fins of lead' and the abstract truth of a
character's reference to 'my cloud of dignity' – for dignity is
something nebulous, that enwraps a person and makes him hard
to see. There is the same sort of pleasing recognition, for me at
least, in mention of 'the murmuring surge' of the sea, in the
worldly truth of the statement that 'There's daggers in men's
smiles,' in Romeo's image of his kiss-ready lips being 'two
blushing pilgrims', or, to give just one more small example, in
Othello's perception that the spirit of vengeance resides in a
'hollow cell'.

One eighteenth-century editor of Shakespeare, Lewis
Theobald, thought the attempt to write about the dramatist
similar to 'going into a large, a spacious, and a splendid dome
through the conveyance of a narrow and obscure entry'. Once
there, 'a glare of light suddenly breaks upon you', and 'a thousand beauties of genius and character, like so many gaudy
apartments pouring at once upon the eye, diffuse and throw
themselves out to the mind'. This prospect, he argued, was 'too
wide to come within the compass of a single view'.

Shakespeare's characters are complex. Many of them are
interesting because they are opaque; their motives, instead of
being transparent, are intriguingly uncertain. There is no better
example of a character who is not transparent than Uncle
Monty's precious Dane. (A fertile ground for speculative bull,
incidentally, is the question of which literary characters are
transparent and which are opaque. It's far from being a lame

issue, but it will appeal to people who like, rather philosophically, to test the consistency of existence.) In a book published more than forty years ago, the Polish drama professor Jan Kott mentioned that 'The bibliography of dissertations and studies devoted to *Hamlet* is twice the size of Warsaw's telephone directory.' I have seen an old Warsaw telephone directory, and Kott's is not a small assertion. Kott also pointed out that the play was 'like a sponge', for it 'absorbs all the problems of our time'. In Michael Almereyda's film of the play, set in twenty-first-century Manhattan, Ethan Hawke's Hamlet is a technophile loafer cut off from humanity by his obsession with filmmaking. He speaks the famous 'To be or not to be' soliloquy while traipsing along the aisles of the local Blockbuster – the section headings blaring at him: 'Action Action Action' – and cleans the murdered courtier Polonius' blood-stained clothes at the laundromat because, like so many New Yorkers, he doesn't have space for a washing machine at home.

A different argument from Kott's is that *Hamlet* is freighted by directors with the problems of our time in order to make it seem fresh. For one of the problems audiences have with the play is that it appears to be full of quotations; the first time you see it, it feels second-hand, because so many phrases from the play – 'brevity is the soul of wit', 'the time is out of joint', 'murder most foul', 'hoist with his own petard', 'neither a borrower nor a lender be' – have seemed, ever since its first performance, so widely applicable. Actors for their part struggle, sometimes too hard, to prevent the familiar from seeming overfamiliar. 'To be or not to be' poses the greatest problem of all, having popped up so often elsewhere – in, just to give a trio of curious examples, Bugs Bunny, *The Mighty Boosh* and an Asterix comic. Frequently,

the soliloquy is spoken by actors as if it is a cliché that needs rean-
imating, and the effects of this can be jarring.

What is it that makes *Hamlet* sponge-like?

To answer this, we have to go back to the original,
Shakespeare's longest play. At the risk of patronizing you, I need
quickly to provide a few details of the plot. If you know them
already, skip the next paragraph.

Hamlet is a Danish prince, son of the recently deceased King
(also called Hamlet) and nephew of the new King, Claudius. At
the start of the play some men on sentry duty believe they have
seen the ghost of the dead King. In due course, Hamlet also sees
this ghostly figure, who reveals that he was murdered by
Claudius. He asks that Hamlet avenge his death, and Hamlet
agrees. Hamlet is not certain about what really happened, but
he is offended by his mother Gertrude's hasty marriage to
Claudius. As he determines first to find out the truth and then
to exact revenge, he procrastinates, cracks jokes, affects madness,
contemplates suicide, and torments his sweetheart Ophelia,
whom he appears to cast as a scapegoat for his mother's supposed
lustfulness. For four hours, there is not much action, and instead
a great deal of talking – getting on for half of it done by Hamlet.

Caught between reason and passion, between the duty to
avenge his father's death and his moral responsibility to avoid
the sin of murder, Hamlet embodies the idea that thinking,
rather than facilitating action, gets in the way of it. 'And thus
the native hue of resolution / Is sicklied o'er with the pale cast
of thought,' he reflects: one's clear-cut instincts are clouded by

judgement. You can make yourself ill with brainwork, says the play; the poet Samuel Taylor Coleridge called it a 'tragedy of thought'. In this, *Hamlet* really does seem 'of our time'. For the first 150 years of its existence, commentators thought it Gothic and antiquated. More recently the fixation with the protagonist, whose psychological turmoil is perceived almost as something independent of the play, has made it seem precocious and radical. Freud went so far as to allege that the play was 'admired for three hundred years without its meaning being discovered'; only with his own theory of the Unconscious, he said, could *Hamlet*'s dramas of repression be truly illuminated.

Even if we are not prepared to go along with Freud, we can see Hamlet as an embodiment of angst. Doubt causes him to unpack his heart. We recognize the way he responds to outrage: impassioned delay. And there are other ways in which he seems contemporary. It is far from easy to tell when he is putting on a performance and when he is being himself. His harsh jokes still feel risqué, as when he asks Ophelia if he can lie in her lap; when she says he should not, he jabs back, 'Do you think I meant country matters?' – embarrassing her by suggesting she misunderstood an innocent question as a sexual proposition. Hamlet is ribald, then, and ingeniously so. He clashes with authority. His university education does not seem to have benefited him practically. In short, he's a slacker, the wrong kind of hero for a drama of revenge. 'There is nothing either good or bad, but thinking makes it so,' he says. This subjectivity – this condition of viewing the world through the medium of one's individuality – isn't something that begins with Hamlet, but it does make him a notable precursor of modern literature's disturbed, melancholy, difficult personalities – and of modern life's. Oddly, the observation was an inspiration for the self-help guru Dale Carnegie, who in *How to Win Friends and Influence People* (1936) quoted it approvingly.

Yet, for all its supposed modernity, *Hamlet* is grounded in earlier sources: a play now lost, possibly by Thomas Kyd; a legend recorded by one François de Belleforest; a Latin account by the historian Saxo Grammaticus. This is typical, for only a few of Shakespeare's plays are not reworkings of existing tales; the plots usually identified as 'original' are those of *The Tempest*, *A Midsummer Night's Dream* and *The Merry Wives of Windsor*. Shakespeare is hardly coy about his use of other people's work. This is worth bearing in mind when you hear commentators insisting that originality is what distinguishes genius from talent. Can refashioning be a kind of genius? How useful, in truth, is the idea of genius?

Most people who would argue for Shakespeare's genius claim that their favourite among his plays is one of *Hamlet*, *King Lear* and *The Tempest*. A nicely contrarian tactic can therefore be to claim a preference for something comparatively obscure. No one will take you seriously if you profess your love of the third part of *Henry VI* – you're just being pranksome – but you could definitely get away with saying you have a special weakness for *Troilus and Cressida* or *The Winter's Tale*.

What are the Top Shakespeare Moments?

I can almost imagine the TV show – three hours, on Channel 4, hosted by Jimmy Carr. Well, maybe not. But you've got some obvious contenders.

1. Cleopatra applying to her breast the fangs of an asp
2. Macbeth's 'Is this a dagger which I see before me?' as he hallucinates
3. Hamlet holding a skull and reflecting 'Alas! poor Yorick. I knew him'
4. Antigonus in *The Winter's Tale* running offstage pursued by a bear
5. Spiteful Iago telling Desdemona's father that she and Othello are 'now making the beast with two backs'

Or what about these?

6. Richard III on the battlefield crying 'A horse! A horse! My kingdom for a horse'
7. In *King Lear*, the blinding of the Earl of Gloucester by his son-in-law, the Duke of Cornwall, who utters the chilling words 'Upon these eyes of thine I'll set my foot'
8. Hamlet hearing Polonius, who is hiding behind a tapestry (known as an 'arras'), and exclaiming 'How now! a rat?' before fatally stabbing him through the arras
9. The monstrous Caliban in *The Tempest* revelling in a list of his island's bounty, which includes such rare things as the toothy little monkey known as the marmoset
10. Juliet stabbing herself with Romeo's dagger and collapsing on his dead body

It would be no crime to say that any of these was your favourite, but I can remember being impressed when someone, years ago, told me that his favourite scene in all of Shakespeare was in *Richard II*, when two gardeners, talking of the monarch's misgovernment, are interrupted by the Queen, who questions them and finds they know rather more about the state of the kingdom than she does. The choice was so surprising that I didn't think to challenge it.

What else do I need to know?

Contrary to what some people imagine, you will not get much credit for trotting out the old line that 'Shakespeare was not written by Shakespeare but by another gentleman of the same name' – or for saying his works were written by someone with a different name. Pretty much no scholar now takes seriously the notions that Shakespeare's plays were penned by Francis Bacon, Queen Elizabeth I, Christopher Marlowe, the sixth Earl of Derby or the seventeenth of Oxford, although the claims of each have been advanced. The idea that the plays were written by someone other than William Shakespeare was apparently first put forward by James Wilmot, a clergyman, in the 1780s, and since then it has magnetized the talents of a succession of cryptographers. Their efforts are characterized by the suspicion that a glove-maker's son could not have produced such great literature. Thus Christmas Humphreys, a lawyer and prolific pamphleteer on arcane subjects: 'It is offensive to . . . our national dignity . . . to worship the memory of a petty-minded tradesman.' This odious drivel is its own rejoinder. Here it will suffice to say that, contrary to what is commonly supposed, there is a huge amount of evidence relating to Shakespeare's life, and there is a wealth of documentation tying this man – an actor, a shareholder in the Globe theatre, a property-owner in Stratford and London – to the authorship of the plays.

Some of what we know of Shakespeare the man is interpreted as presenting him in a less than favourable light. In his will, for instance, he provided that his wife Anne Hathaway should be left his 'second-best bed'. This has been interpreted as callous, a rubbish souvenir, a deliberate insult. But of course, it's quite plausible that the second-best bed was the one he had actually slept in with his wife, the best bed being kept for guests, and its associations could therefore have been affectionate.

One reason why imputations of bad character may be awkward is that Shakespeare has repeatedly been exploited as a symbol of Britishness. Just opening my wallet, I find his image on my debit card, and for many years it appeared on the £20 banknote. Yet he is hardly a British preserve, having been translated into a vast number of languages, including Basque, Maori, Esperanto and Zulu. It is not just in Stratford, but also in Verona, that the tourist industry has embraced his stories. (Visitors to what is alleged to be Juliet's House on Verona's Via Cappello can touch the breast of a bronze Juliet, hoping for some of the romantic magic, or add their amorous graffiti to the already copious collection on the walls.) Shakespeare and his characters have been used to market cigars, soft drinks and petrol, and have adorned pub signs, chess sets and the names of public spaces.

Ten 'socially useful' Shakespeare quotations

1. For a moment when the right expression of pleasure escapes you: 'Silence is the perfectest herald of joy: I

were but little happy, if I could say how much' (Claudio in *Much Ado About Nothing*)

2. When you don't want someone to think your approval of a person is all that strong: 'My meaning in saying he is a good man, is, to have you understand me that he is sufficient' (Shylock in *The Merchant of Venice*)

3. When plotting: 'Look like the innocent flower, / But be the serpent under it' (Lady Macbeth)

4. When there isn't enough time to make the most of meeting somebody: 'Hereafter, in a better world than this, / I shall desire more love and knowledge of you' (Le Beau in *As You Like It*)

5. If the kids are playing up: 'How sharper than a serpent's tooth it is / To have a thankless child!' (King Lear)

6. To express one's feelings of resignation when no cure for one's problems is at hand: 'The miserable have no other medicine, / But only hope' (Claudio in *Measure for Measure*)

7. To be said with great theatre, if you find yourself getting thrown in a river, or indeed on any other occasion when you want to get some humour out of a fall: 'You may know by my size, that I have a kind of alacrity in sinking' (Falstaff in *The Merry Wives of Windsor*)

8. Faced with being overlooked in favour of someone more physically attractive: 'What, is the jay more precious than the lark, / Because his feathers are more beautiful?' (Petruchio in *The Taming of the Shrew*)

9. When the space of life seems more than usually short: 'I wasted time, and now doth time waste me' (Richard II in the play of that name)

10. To drive home the point that names are just meaningless conventions: 'What's in a name? That which we call a rose, / By any other word would smell as sweet' (Juliet in *Romeo and Juliet*)

Not without a certain irony, the best films of Shakespeare are, in many critics' eyes, those of the Japanese director Akira Kurosawa; *Ran* adapts the story of *King Lear*, while *Throne of Blood* follows *Macbeth*. Neither contains a single phrase of Shakespeare's original, and both radically alter the Shakespearean plots. Besides the many quite orthodox films of the plays, there are radical retellings. Lloyd Kaufman's *Tromeo and Juliet* includes bizarre dismemberments, incest and a lesbian romp involving Juliet and the Nurse. More accessibly, Enzo Castellari's *Johnny Hamlet* translates Shakespeare's most famous tragedy into the idiom of the spaghetti Western; *The Tempest* has been reworked as *Forbidden Planet* and *Age of Consent*; Gus van Sant's *My Own Private Idaho* updates the two parts of *Henry IV*; Gil Junger's *10 Things I Hate About You* does the same for *The Taming of the Shrew*; and the *Godfather* trilogy pays tacit homage to the story of *King Lear*, while John Boorman's *Where the Heart Is* does so more obviously. Plenty more examples could be adduced. These films are considered by some to be travesties, mere provocations; they flourish the rhetorical question 'Did you ever imagine Shakespeare could be like *this*?' But it is striking that so many filmmakers bother with such adaptation and allusions. They are tributes to the size of Shakespeare's shadow.

Shakespeare was prescient in his understanding of how long-lived literature can be. 'Not marble nor the gilded monuments / Of princes shall outlive this pow'rful rhyme,' he wrote. The lines are from one of his sonnets – love poems that have indeed lasted far longer than the love of which they speak and a host of gilded monuments. Good stuff for a Valentine's card, you might think, but tread carefully. These 154 playful fourteen-line poems were written for circulation among Shakespeare's 'private friends', possibly at a moment when the theatres were closed because of an outbreak of plague and the poet had time on his hands.

In his plays, Shakespeare disparages sonnets; they are trite devices, 'wailful' instruments of wooing. In turning to the form, he may well have been trying to freshen up the stale conventions of love poetry. His take on the sonnet is in many ways unusual. Most of the 154 little poems are addressed to a young man, who is not named; all but one of the first 17 urge this young man to marry and procreate, and the next 109 present Shakespeare's relationship with him. In several of the sonnets, roughly halfway through the sequence, there are references to a rival poet – perhaps the flamboyant Christopher Marlowe, or a composite of several rivals to Shakespeare, including another dramatist, Ben Jonson. Only the last twenty-eight of the sonnets are directly concerned with heterosexual desire, in this case for a nameless woman identified several times as 'black' (and consequently known as the 'dark lady', although she is only once called 'dark' in the poems). One of the overall effects of the sequence is to suggest that Shakespeare himself was bisexual, although these enigmatic poems are more aptly described as 'homosocial' than as 'homosexual'. Attempts to decipher the identity of the young man and black lady have been many and laborious. The man is thought to have been Henry Wriothesley, who was Earl of Southampton, or another nobleman, William Herbert, Earl of Pembroke. The so-called dark lady may have been the poet Emilia Lanier (also known as Emilia Bassano), or a woman who kept a brothel and was known as Black Lucy, or a royal servant, Mary Fitton.

Whether or not the sonnets reproduce episodes from real life, their emotional force is a given. Some readers behave as if they are a novel, a single narrative about a love triangle, rich in the drama of desire, friendship, betrayal and death. Admirers of these poems find, as with so much writing they think good, that it can be hard to identify what exactly it is they like about them. There is something at once delicate and simple about the lines 'Like as the waves make towards the pebbled shore, / So do our minutes hasten to their end' – but spot the play on the words 'our minutes' (hour, minutes) – and there is something deliciously filthy in the lines 'Take heed, dear heart, of this large privilege; / The hardest knife ill used doth lose his edge' – a man's large, hard 'privilege', if he's recklessly promiscuous, can become less robust, less impressive.

Nine more things to know about Shakespeare

1. None of his manuscripts has survived.
2. His plays are usually grouped in the categories tragedy, comedy and history. The history play is Shakespeare's invention, but it is the comedies which are the most numerous, and they almost always involve mistaken identity, with several of them also involving cross-dressing.

3. It is believed that he wrote two plays that have been lost, *Cardenio* and *Love's Labour's Won*.

4. London's Globe Theatre was built in 1599 and burnt down in 1613. It was rebuilt the following year, closing in 1642. The modern reconstruction, completed in 1997, is about 200 yards from the original site. There have been several other replicas around the world, including two in Texas.

5. Although Shakespeare was only fifty-two when he died, he had already retired from writing.

6. Contemporary documents show as many as eighty-three different spellings of his name.

7. His longest play, *Hamlet*, is two and a quarter times longer than his shortest, *The Comedy of Errors*.

8. Quotations from his plays have provided the titles of many other books, including Vladimir Nabokov's *Pale Fire* (from *Timon of Athens*), Aldous Huxley's *Brave New World* (*The Tempest*), Thomas Hardy's *Under the Greenwood Tree* (*As You Like It*), William Faulkner's *The Sound and the Fury* (*Macbeth*) and Frederick Forsyth's *The Dogs of War* (*Julius Caesar*).

9. Shakespeare's first child, Susanna, was only the sixth girl in Stratford to be baptized with that name. His two other children, twins, were named for their godparents, Hamnet and Judith Sadler. Hamnet Shakespeare died aged eleven, of causes unknown.

―――――◆―――――

So, should you send one of Shakespeare's sonnets as a Valentine? Perhaps not. They're too radical, too unstable and too contentious for such purposes. The sonnets are as close as we ever get to what Shakespeare thought, but still we are a long way from knowing precisely what he did think. As one of my teachers used to say, all you can be sure of is that he *did* think, and – related to this – there's a law that, whatever you think of, Shakespeare will have thought of it first.

It is as well to remember that Shakespeare's status, his currency, his visibility, relies on an industry – of filmmakers, publishers and impresarios, to name a few – who believe they can make money out of his works and his image. Shakespeare is obviously not alone in this, but let's be clear: there are commercial reasons, as well as political ones, why some authors are lionized. So is Shakespeare timeless? The answer, I believe, is that he is, because his ways of thinking are fundamental. By this I mean that he has the courage to ask simple questions, especially about people, and brings to bear on them an intelligence that is not just a product of his historical circumstances. It is fashionable to say that works of literature betray the conditions of the time in which they were written, and to say that a writer is an 'effect' of an environment. Shakespeare shows that the act of making art can be altogether more mysterious than that. It contains a suggestion of divinity that takes us back to the Creation myth itself.

How to talk to an actor about Shakespeare

Many of us know people who act. I'm not suggesting that you are bosom buddies with Hollywood royalty, but simply that you will have friends or relatives (a niece, a cousin, an acquaintance from school) who goes in for 'am dram' or has wrestled with the role of Second Spear-carrier. Anyone serious about acting will sooner or later essay Shakespeare, but it is a rare actor who looks at a speech in a Shakespeare play and finds that it leaps off the page fully armed with drama and meaning. So ask your actor what the process is that brings to life the charisma of the lines.

Bear in mind, too, that professional actors are more likely than just about anyone else to question the plays' authorship. Why? Because actors are especially attuned to the ensemble effort that is involved in creating theatre. The idea that the plays were conceived not by an individual, but by a group – including actors – appeals to their sense of the fertile possibilities of collaboration.

When it comes to chitchat with an actor, unless you want to go down the obnoxious route of complaining about how mannered and self-conscious modern performers' interpretations of Shakespeare are, or about how poor their diction is, flatter his or her ego by exploring the techniques through which a character, be it Lady Macbeth or a lowly messenger, is created. How, and in what proportions, do they use research, imitation and observation?

8

WHAT'S ACTUALLY IN THE BIBLE?

There are more unread copies of the Bible than of any other book. This statement, uttered by a Christian, conveys the impression that knowledge of the Bible is in crisis. But the large number of unread Bibles is a result of Christians' ambitiously wide transmission of their sacred text. It is estimated that twenty million copies are distributed each year, and that about thirty times as many extracts from it are handed out. The whole Bible has been translated into around 400 languages, and sections of it into more than 2,000. To put this in perspective: there have been authorized translations of the Harry Potter novels into about sixty languages, and when I referred earlier to Shakespeare being translated into a 'vast' number of languages, the estimates range between 80 and 118.

The Bible is a source not only of religious teachings, but also of political authority, practical guidance and some of the most potent symbolism in both high and low culture. To some it is a compendium of valuable moral teachings: to others a repository of historical truths. It is has been described as a 'great confused novel' (by the novelist D. H. Lawrence), 'the most beautiful book in the world' (by the usually acerbic essayist

H. L. Mencken), and as 'a warrant for trafficking in humans, for ethnic cleansing, for slavery, for bride price, and indiscriminate massacre' (by Christopher Hitchens, in his recent *God Is Not Great*). There is no written work that, over the history of its existence, has proved more forceful or more divisive. It is also, as I have found, taken quite literally be people whose lifestyle would seem to make it hard to do so.

'God didn't create the world in six days so you could use language like that,' I was once informed, after uttering some very mild profanity – I had stripped the skin off the tip of one of my fingers, buying the *San Francisco Chronicle* from a vending machine, and, as I waited in line for a chance to eat the best French toast in the North Beach area, found myself being rebuked by a woman who resembled Shirley MacLaine. I did not expect this in San Francisco. In fact, I would not expect it anywhere. I've been secularized, and I am not used to having the name of God invoked against me. Yet indirectly it happens all the time.

According to a survey conducted in 2007 by the California-based Barna Group, a company whose goal is to provide information and resources to 'help facilitate spiritual transformation in America', more than 50 per cent of Americans do actually believe that the universe was created in six days, and there are as many who accept that Moses physically parted the Red Sea, and that Jesus Christ rose from the dead after being crucified and buried. Such a literal reading of the Bible, pushed to its limit, involves accepting that the world is flat and is supported on pillars, and that the sun goes round the earth.

I've just referred several times to the Bible in the singular. But the Bible is not really a single book. Rather, it is a collection of books by many (human) authors, written over about 1,500 years. Its material is diverse: Jews originally spoke of 'the Scrolls', Christians of 'the Books'. This is hardly trivial; the question of which books properly belong in the Hebrew Bible, and of which belong in the Christian Bible, has been keenly debated. For convenience's sake, we refer to the Bible as something static – and in the singular. And to believers, its singularity is doctrinally important. The Bible's existence as a single volume suggests that it is a coherent body of teachings, stable and elsewhere unavailable – a Christian constitution, the Word of God.

Christians derive from the Bible a set of moral instructions. To non-believers, the centrality in Christians' lives of the Bible's

---

Five curious verses in the Bible (Authorized Version)

1. 'For she [Aholibah] doted upon their paramours, whose flesh is as the flesh of asses, and whose issue is like the issue of horses' (Ezekiel 23.20)

2. 'A word fitly spoken is like apples of gold in pictures of silver' (Proverbs 25.11)

3. 'Let your women keep silence in the churches: for it is not permitted unto them to speak; but they are commanded to be under obedience, as also saith the law' (1 Corinthians 14.34)

4. 'Yet these may ye eat of every flying creeping thing that goeth upon all four, which have legs above their feet, to leap withal upon the earth' (Leviticus 11.21)

5. 'He that is wounded in the stones, or hath his privy member cut off, shall not enter into the congregation of the Lord' (Deuteronomy 23.1)

---

directives becomes apparent when conversation turns to subjects such as homosexuality, justice, abortion and natural history. The Bible provides other, less binding guidance. For instance, the Book of Ecclesiastes argues that a sincere life of small religious observances is better than an overstretched attempt at large accomplishments, while in the Book of Proverbs there are suggestive, riddling observations. A personal favourite is this: 'There be three things which are too wonderful for me, yea, four which I know not: the way of an eagle in the air; the way of a serpent upon a rock; the way of a ship in the midst of the sea; and the way of a man with a maid.'

The Bible's critics contend that the words of guidance are contradictory and, more disturbingly, are intermingled with examples of depravity and abuse. It is true that the Bible contains scenes of remarkable violence. In *The God Delusion* Richard Dawkins cites some of the most shocking: the episode in the Book of Judges where a priest's concubine is raped, dies, and is then cut up into pieces by the priest; or the more famous one in the Book of Genesis where Lot, advised by angels to leave the doomed town of Sodom, tries to appease the locals who want to rape the angels by offering them instead his virginal daughters (who later have sex with him when he is drunk). I have seen one estimate suggesting that the Old Testament contains 600 incidents of human violence and, more to the point, almost twice as many of divine violence. This sort of thing sits uncomfortably in a work of moral teaching. To many it suggests a brutal, vain and vengeful God. Dawkins describes the God of the Old Testament as 'a misogynist, pestilential, megalomaniacal, sadomasochistic, capriciously malevolent bully'. He's not exactly mincing his words. The New

Testament is sometimes presented as an antidote to the Old Testament's savagery, but it too is full of violent language and violent acts. Moreover, the Bible has been used to provide theological justification for all manner of barbaric practices, such as genocide, slavery, the subordination of women, inquisitions, witch burnings, and apartheid in South Africa.

Among Christians, though, there is a view that the horrors of the Bible are a diagnosis of the pervasiveness of violence. The Bible lets them see what kind of world they inhabit. Once the violence is understood, it becomes possible to see beyond it. Why does evil happen? To teach us to value its alternatives. John Milton argued, 'There is evil in the world because God in his generosity wished his creatures to be free.' He went on to say that 'the obedience of a predetermined puppet, a creature that *cannot* sin, is wholly without moral life; the obedience of a free agent, exposed to darkness, danger, pain and sin, is morally real because it is alive'. So, the Bible's episodes of savagery are a tutorial in freedom. Believers argue forcefully that, complete with all these brutal moments, the Bible can irrigate the mind. They draw attention to its teachings about the importance of forgiveness, humility and kindness, as well as to the way it promotes ideas of community and love, argues the need for hard work, and provides people with an ethical structure for their lives.

For present purposes, however, I want to emphasize that the Bible is a work of literature – we might compare it to the *Iliad* – and suggest you can take an interest in its contents without having to acknowledge their truth. The Bible's authors did not think of it in such terms, and neither, of course, do Christians. Yet even if you are sure that Christianity deserves to fade away, and even if you are repulsed by those heaven-bound paragons of piety who seem completely detached from the real world, there is much in the Bible that can be savoured on aesthetic grounds alone: great stories, for instance, like Jonah getting swallowed by the whale, or David doing battle with Goliath.

If it's possible to delight in the Bible's uplifting incidents, it's also possible, especially if you are a fan of *Resident Evil* or Steven Seagal, to revel in the less savoury ones: Samson catching 300 foxes and shortly afterwards killing a thousand men with the jawbone of an ass; the two female bears in the second Book of Kings that maul forty-two youths; and Shamgar, a judge, striking down 600 Philistines with a stick he'd otherwise have used to prod oxen. These details are not edifying, but they stay in the mind, like the highlights of an action film. Even Richard Dawkins can concede that the Bible is 'an arresting and poetic work of fiction'.

That word 'poetic' seems apposite. The Bible brims with poetry. There are aphorisms, there is majestic language, and there are gorgeously expressive passages. In the Book of Isaiah, for instance, we can read about the end of time, when God's chosen will come 'out of all nations upon horses, and in chariots, and in litters, and upon mules, and upon swift beasts, to my holy mountain Jerusalem'. Jerusalem itself is portrayed as a mother, and the people who dwell there will 'be satisfied with the breasts of her consolations': 'then shall ye suck, ye shall be borne upon her sides, and shall be dandled upon her knees'. Elsewhere, there is a fine simplicity: 'All flesh is as grass, and all the glory of man as the flower of grass' (in other words, enjoy life while you can, and be aware that triumph is fleeting), 'Let not the sun go down upon your wrath' (if you're angry, try and sort it out before you go to bed), 'A man that flattereth his neighbour spreadeth a net for his feet' (which is surely self-explanatory) and 'A good name is better than precious ointment' (again, self-explanatory).

The King James Bible, from which these quotations come, has fertilized the language of everyday speech. Take the expressions 'good and faithful servant', 'O ye of little faith', 'thirty pieces of silver', 'our daily bread', 'the salt of the earth', 'an eye for an eye and a tooth for a tooth', 'out of the mouths of babes', 'the blind lead the blind', 'seek and ye shall find' and 'no man can serve two masters': all are from the King James Bible. In fact, every single one of them appears in its version of St Matthew's Gospel – just one book among many. And to the earlier translation by William Tyndale, a sixteenth-century reformer who ended up being burnt at the stake, we owe the seemingly timeless turns of phrase 'blessed are the peacemakers', 'the signs of the times', 'let there be light' and 'eat, drink, and be merry'.

As a source of morality, the Bible does not seem, to the dispassionate observer, exemplary. But it is solemnly recognized by people we encounter every day as an inspired work of revelation, and the vocabulary with which it equips us, whatever we think of its import, permeates our daily speech. It hardly seems controversial to say that it is the most significant book in the history of Western civilization and the major source of European culture. William Blake pronounced that 'The Old and New Testaments are the Great Code of Art'. Many people will resist this type of claim. But try and name a book – or indeed anything else – that has wielded greater influence. You do not need to be susceptible to this influence in order to accept that it exists.

However, there are other religious texts which today seem to wield a more immediate influence. This is nowhere more clear than in the case of the Qur'an – a work quite similar in content to the Bible, with which it shares many themes and characters, yet far more revered and also far more feared. The ascendancy of the Qur'an seems a fact of modern life. Its character needs exploring.

9

HOW DO YOU TALK ABOUT THE QUR'AN?

If you are not a Muslim, *carefully*. Or perhaps, if you are keen to stay out of trouble, not at all. Talking about the sacred texts of any religion is dangerous, and there is a tendency for people to disparage the texts of religions to which they do not subscribe. They look in them for things that sound stupid. Critics of political Islam like nothing more than to use the Qur'an as evidence of Muslims' supposed imbecility. They may cite the verse which states that 'men are the managers of the affairs of women' or hold up to ridicule the requirement that an adulterer be given a hundred lashes – both in fact subjects of debate and dispute among Muslims. It is common to hear someone assert that the Qur'an is 'sick', or that it incites violence, advocates terrorism and is hatefully misogynistic. Statements of this kind are typically made by people who have never looked inside the Qur'an.

A change of angle, to exemplify this. I am at a cricket match, and I fall into conversation with a fellow beer-drinker at the bar. 'The thing about Pakistan', he tells me, 'is they see sport as jihad.' I ask him what jihad is. 'Holy war. Everyone knows that.' And where do the Pakistani cricketers get their idea of jihad? 'It's in their holy book, isn't it!' I ask what it actually says because, you know, I'm curious. My fellow beer-drinker throws his head back – laughing in an evasive way I recognize. 'That I don't know.' He pauses. 'But you've only got to read the papers to see it – every day. *Islamic fundamentalism*. It's a disease, mate.'

Whenever anyone claims 'It says in the Qur'an . . .' – as in 'It says in the Qur'an that it's a sin to tell a joke' – be sceptical. The prevalence of myths about Islamic teachings is one of a whole raft of reasons for having a closer knowledge of the Qur'an and its contents. Recent world events have made this need seem urgent to many who have neither a direct connection with Islam nor any interest in its spiritual message. Why and how is this sacred text such an inspiration? What does it actually have to say about how a Muslim should conduct his or her life? Few Muslims will pretend that they fully understand the Qur'an, or are able to perceive all its subtleties, and many will concede that they do not find everything in it attractive, but a large part of what it contains is much less alien to non-Muslims, ethically and practically, than its detractors tend to make out.

The Qur'an is the mainstay of Islam, its core. It provides Muslims with a worldview, amd they regard it as the literal, infallible and inimitable word of God (the Arabic word for God being Allah). Written in Arabic, it speaks with a big voice – one which creates for Muslims a whole rhetoric grounded in religious faith. In the original, it is a rhapsodic feat of prose, a mixture of dramatic narrative, dialogue, short revelatory sentences, oaths concerning its own validity, exhortations and injunctions, abounding with rhymes, patterns, similes, intensifying adjectives and fecund ambiguities: in translation, even at its most sympathetic, the rhetorical power is lost. The first translations were created in order to give non-Muslims the opportunity to refute its teachings, and some of the more recent ones have apparently underplayed its scriptural meaning. (In any case, Muslims regard such translations as travesties. There is only one Qur'an, and it is in Arabic.) The Qur'an exists to be read aloud; its name means 'recitation' or 'recital'. To those who know no Arabic, it is a work of literature, static and occasionally thunderous: to Muslims, it is alive. In one popular image, its words are the twigs of a burning bush that is aflame with God. Moreover, it is thanks to the Qur'an that Arabic has travelled far beyond its heartland in the Arabian peninsula.

The word *Islam* means 'submission', and the practice of Islam is not simply a profession of belief, but a total surrender to the will of God. Islam is a religion, but it is more than that – a way of life – and the Qur'an furnishes Muslims with a set of principles by which to live. Many have recourse to the Qur'an on a daily basis; for instance, a parent may choose to recite verses at the bedside of an ailing child, and a business venture or public meeting may be initiated with a similar recitation.

One of the most common misconceptions about Islam is that its god is Muhammad. In fact, Muhammad, though deeply venerated, was the last in a line of prophets sent to expound divine wisdom to mankind. The prophets who preceded him were Adam, Noah, Abraham, Moses and Jesus. Muhammad, the so-called sixth legislator, restored the integrity of a faith which had become corrupted. He was the messenger, not the message or its author, and Muslims consider it blasphemous to say that Muhammad wrote the Qur'an. The Qur'an is understood to emanate from God, and it is this God, who explains himself to people through his prophets, that Muslims worship.

The standard belief is that a revelation came to Muhammad while he was meditating in a cave near the city of Mecca. This happened in AD 610, at which time he was forty years old. Muhammad had no track record as a poet or orator; he was inspired by divine messages, unfolded to him by the spirit Gabriel, and there are more than 200 references in the Qur'an to its contents being 'sent down' to the Prophet. The process of revelation continued bit by bit for twenty-three years, and each fresh revelation was written down by scribes (ultimately twenty-nine in number) to whom Muhammad dictated the verses. After Muhammad's death in 632, the revelations were gathered into a single volume by the leader of the Islamic state, Abu Bakr.

As news of the revelations spread in the years following Muhammad's experience in the cave, pilgrims began to travel to Mecca. But as this happened his followers increasingly found themselves persecuted or ostracized. Eventually, after the death of his wife Khadija, Muhammad relocated to Yathrib, about 250 miles to the north of Mecca, and his followers migrated there too. At Yathrib he built the first Islamic mosque, and the growing Muslim community there came to be known simply by the name Medina (meaning 'city'). Mecca and Medina remain the two key holy sites of Islam; both are in modern-day Saudi Arabia. Extensive renovation of the sites was carried out in the twentieth century; the construction company responsible was run by Mohammed bin Laden, a Yemeni immigrant among whose fifty-four children was Osama, 'the lion', of whom we have all since heard a great deal.

Muslims are required to make the pilgrimage to Mecca at least once in their lives. This is one of the so-called pillars of Islam: the others are declaring faith in God, fasting during the month of Ramadan, giving alms once a year, and performing *salat* (worship) five times a day. Recitation from the Qur'an is crucial to the last of these, and devout Muslims aspire to know their sacred book intimately. Yet, as the mystic theologian al-Ghazali noted, it is a 'deep sea' and cannot be exhausted. There is no Islamic 'church' in the sense that there is, say, a Roman Catholic Church overseen by the Pope, and the raw materials of the Qur'an have been explained and given structure by scholars and apologists, not by a single overarching institution. Meanwhile, among non-Muslims, who tend to have very little idea of what the book contains, scurrilous myths abound. Let me give one example.

It is sometimes alleged that there is a verse in the Qur'an which promises that those who die in the name of Islam will be rewarded with the opportunity to deflower seventy-two virgins. One claim that results from this is that male Muslim suicide bombers wrap their penises in muslin to keep them clean in readiness for their heavenly feast of carnality. Another is that the line actually refers not to seventy-two virgins, but to seventy-two glasses of wine. This is all garbage.

In the Qur'an the riches of paradise – which will be enjoyed by all Muslims who have done good deeds, rather than just by martyrs – are conveyed more than once and in considerable detail. Those who reach paradise will recline on pleasant couches – jewelled, or possibly brocaded – and be brought delicious beverages and fruit, and they will have loving companions to attend to their desires. In the widely distributed translation by N. J. Dawood, an Iraqi, we read also that 'They shall sit with bashful, dark-eyed virgins, as chaste as the sheltered eggs of ostriches,' and later that these virgins are 'as fair as corals and rubies' and are 'sheltered in their tents'. A more recent version by Muhammad Abdel Haleem describes the virgins being 'good-natured', 'sheltered in pavilions' and 'modest of gaze'.

Translations of these passages are contentious. In some versions, these dark-eyed virgins are identified as angels. In others they have swelling breasts. Moreover, a recent and acclaimed work of German scholarship has argued that the particular kind of bliss on offer is indeed nothing more mouth-watering than an array of chilled drinks. Still, whichever reading you accept, the figure seventy-two is conspicuous by its absence. It crops up only in later commentaries – notably one by the fifteenth-century teacher al-Suyuti, who explains that in paradise one can experience an eternal erection and ready access to enticing vaginas. Al-Suyuti's interpretation has been influential, but in the Qur'an the emphasis is on purity, not sensual excess: there are thirty-four references to the waters that flow beneath paradise, cleansing it, and instead of talk there is the sublime babble of a fountain. In any case, there is far more about spiritual rewards than about tangible ones, and the picture of the material bounty of paradise is identified as *mathal* – a parable of what it will be like to enjoy the hereafter, rather than a list of the fixtures and fittings the righteous will find there.

This whole issue of what the Qur'an does and doesn't say is inflammatory. Non-Muslims use their typically very sketchy knowledge of the Qur'an to bolster claims about the nature of Islam and the character of Muslims. Can you comfortably generalize about a billion people? Most of us will think not. And as

for making assumptions based on a brisk and incomplete reading of the Qur'an, we can surely recognize the dangers of this,
not least because its contents mean different things according to
who you are and where you are.

Five further misconceptions about the Qur'an

1. *It urges Muslims to slaughter non-believers 'wherever you find them'*. In fact, the Qur'an urges Muslims to fight only in self-defence or to defend oppressed people who ask for their help.

2. *It is scientifically primitive.* On the contrary, there are pas-sages in the Qur'an which suggest that the origin of life on earth is aquatic, allude to sexual reproduction in plants, describe the development of the human embryo, and even hint at the circulation of blood in the body.

3. *It contains a so-called 'sword verse' urging Muslims to kill people who believe in other gods.* In fact, the people in ques-tion are those who have explicitly been hostile to Islam and have prevented others from becoming Muslims.

4. *It encourages polygamy.* The Qur'an permits a man to take as many as four wives, but emphasizes that he must avoid bias and should take only one wife if there is a risk that by taking more he will fail to treat his wives equitably.

5. *It rubbishes the Christian Bible.* Actually, it addresses Christians and Jews, telling them the 'good news' that salvation is at hand. Just dipping into the Qur'an, one may be struck by the references to Adam and Eve, Abraham, Joseph, Jonah, Mary the mother of Jesus, and Jesus himself.

The Qur'an consists of 114 sections – each section known as a *sura* (literally, a 'row'). These are sometimes spoken of as though they are chapters, but this is misleading, as a *sura* can comprise anywhere between a single line and 286 verses. In all, the 114 *suras* contain about 6,200 verses. These do not make up a continuous narrative, and the structure is not obviously logical. Questions of belief, morality and ethics sit side by side with legal provisions and teachings about ritual practices. Guidance is offered through a mixture of *tarhib* – which consists of encouraging the fear of doing evil – and *targhib* – which involves arousing the desire to do good. Words of intimidation are thus balanced by inducements, which is a pattern familiar to most sports coaches, bosses, teachers and parents.

This 'mother of all books', as it is known, is the word of God, and at the same time much of it is about God. The most fundamental assertion of the Qur'an is the 'oneness' of God – his uniqueness, eternity, power, self-sufficiency and need of neither partner nor patron. In addition, many other characteristics are emphasized: God's mercy, omniscience, role as a guide to spiritual and practical matters, power over life and death, and judicious reckoning.

Nevertheless, one of the things that may well be spotted by someone who reads the Qur'an straight through is that it appears to contradict itself. Take, for instance, its references to wine. The fruits of the vine are praised, but they are also condemned as one of the 'abominations devised by Satan' (others are games of chance, idols and 'divining arrows'). It is this apparent contradictoriness that lies behind the complexity of Islamic jurisprudence. Muslim jurists have to use reason, analogy, interpretative skill and reference to precedent – a set of techniques known as *fiqh* – in order to arrive at their rulings.

Here are some more examples of the sort of thing you can find in the Qur'an. Profane talk should be avoided, and alms should be given to the poor. It is forbidden to eat the flesh of pigs, carrion, or any animal strangled or beaten to death. Offensive nicknames are also forbidden. Marriage is encouraged, and children are a special divine gift. Adultery is a cardinal sin. Fasting is prescribed to test believers' self-restraint. The correct practice, on encountering unbelievers on the battlefield, is to strike off their heads. Before prayer, believers should wash their faces, their hands and their arms up to the elbow, and should wipe their heads and the feet up as far as the ankle, and if they can find no water they should use sand. Some of this may seem odd, but much of it does not.

Perhaps more than anything, though, it is the contemporary buzzword *jihad* that shapes popular ideas about what the Qur'an stands for. The essential business of *jihad* is self-purification: *jihad* is an act of spiritual engagement, a kind of striving or struggle against evil, rather than holy war. In practice, however, it tends to mean warfare. Thus, for instance, Osama bin Laden's statement in an interview with the CNN reporter Peter Arnett in March 1997 that 'We declared *jihad* against the US government, because the US government is unjust, criminal, and tyrannical.'

In the second chapter of the Qur'an we read (again this is Dawood's translation): 'Fight for the sake of God those that fight against you, but do not attack them first. God does not love aggressors.' As for fighting between different Muslim factions, the Qur'an is explicit that Muslims are a band of brothers, and every Muslim has a duty to make peace when there is discord among fellow believers. Yet there *are* passages that invoke violence against unbelievers. 'For those that disbelieve in God and His apostle,' it is explained in the 48th *sura*, 'We have prepared a blazing Fire for the unbelievers.' Herein lies the seed of the myth that violence can be an act of redemption. It's worth noting that religious metaphors – and not just those of Islam – are commonly violent. Belief is represented as a fight, and religious rituals act out or recall traumas.

But let's go back to the cricket. 'It's a disease, mate.' Pints are finished; more drinks are ordered. The disease is what exactly? 'The whole thing. They're hooked on war – it's in their book.' It's worse than the Bible? 'That I couldn't tell you. But why don't you stop with the questions and watch the game?' After a pause, there is an ambiguous afterthought: 'There's everything still to play for, isn't there?'

Interpreting the Qur'an is difficult, as every Muslim knows. One of the key reasons is the Qur'an's pluralism – its in-built awareness of diversity. The negative image of the Qur'an that circulates among a significant part of the non-Muslim world is a distortion and is ideologically motivated. Karen Armstrong, one of the leading experts in comparative religion, has emphasized the dangers of this: 'We can no longer afford to indulge this type of bigotry, because it is a gift to extremists who can use . . . [it] to "prove" that the Western world is indeed engaged on a new crusade against the Islamic world.' But some of the distortions begin with the militants. Most Muslims think of their faith as pacific and mystical, and one of the reasons for the upsurge in political Islam is that globalization and the modernity it brings are causing many Muslims to become increasingly secular in their habits. The hard-liners are fighting this tendency, and in doing so they invoke the Qur'an. Ironically, their brand of ideology is informed not just by the Qur'an, but by other influences from European political philosophers such as Karl Marx, and, not so ironically, the bigotry to which Karen Armstrong refers is something they are keen to drum up.

This has been a sober chapter, for reasons I do not need to labour, but, in keeping with the spirit of my book, I'll end on a lighter note with a digression. In the Qur'an, the honey bee is discussed in some detail. Bees are claimed to have been inspired by God to build their nests in the hills, in trees or in hives constructed by men, and 'from their bellies comes a drink of different colours, wherein there is healing for the people'. According to the nineteenth-century explorer Sir Richard Burton, there were eight or nine different varieties of honey to be found in Mecca. 'The Arabs,' he wrote, 'are curious in, and fond of, honey,' and 'the best, and in Arab parlance the "coldest", is the green kind, produced by bees that feed upon a thorny plant called "Sihhah".'

10

CAN PROUST CHANGE YOUR LIFE?

Proust lived 1871–1922.

Major work: *À la recherche du temps perdu* (begun 1909, finished 1922). There is controversy over the correct English translation of the book's title – see later in this chapter.

Also wrote: *Contre Sainte-Beuve*, an essay pouring scorn on an influential literary critic, and *Jean Santeuil*, a novel which he abandoned, in which he tried out some of the material that later appeared in *À la recherche*.

Trivia: Proust's most intense relationship was with his chauffeur and secretary Alfred Agostinelli. After one of Agostinelli's many dalliances with other people (mainly women), Proust tried to lure him back with lavish gifts – a Rolls-Royce and an aeroplane. Agostinelli, who was keen to become a pilot, declined both gifts, but continued to take flying lessons. Soon afterwards he died after crashing a plane in the sea near Antibes; he may well have been attacked by sharks.

It may seem strange to move from the Qur'an to Marcel Proust, but the two have something in common. For when people speak of Proust (whose name rhymes with *roost*), they are thinking of *À la recherche du temps perdu*, a book which has a legitimate claim to be the least read of literary classics. It and the Qur'an may well be the books most often alluded to by people who have never read a single page of them.

For a while now I've been casually noting references in the media to Marcel Proust and his writings. Consequently, I can disclose that he is the favourite author of the Texan ex-model Jerry Hall, and a favourite also of Vivienne Westwood, Donna Tartt and Elie Wiesel. Among the phenomena I've seen described as Proustian have been part of the cartoon movie *Ratatouille*, a girl scout badge, the journalistic efforts of Mary-Kate Olsen, a record sleeve, Germolene, a substantial biography of John Maynard Keynes, the military associations of luncheon meat, a rice pudding, images of Blackpool, and the smell of an Afghan coat.

This alone might be enough to put you off. Proust's masterpiece is one of those books people are always meaning to get round to – a line we instantly recognize as specious. Those who haven't done so refer to it as they would to a mythical beast. Furthermore, it is the perfect example of a book with a high drop-out rate; for every fifty people who start it, only one reaches the end. I am guessing here, and it may be that I am too generous in this estimate.

À la recherche in fact consists of seven volumes, published between 1913 and 1927. It is sometimes described as a *roman fleuve*; this term, literally meaning a 'river novel', signifies a sequence of books which, taken together, chronicle an entire period or society through the lives of a family or community. Although the seven volumes of *À la recherche* are often regarded just as a single large novel, they do exactly this, concentrating on the lives of aristocrats, their hangers-on, courtesans, society artists and servants, and quietly showing the impact of technology on manners, social habits and perception.

Roger Shattuck, in his valuable short book *Proust's Binoculars*, captures the experience of reading it, which 'is like looking at a map on which one sees clearly the names of all the cities and rivers and principal provinces, but not the name of the country itself'. In a more recent study, Shattuck says that 'reading Proust bears many resemblances to visiting a zoo', as 'the specimens he collected from the remotest corners of society amaze and amuse us in their variety'. These specimens include the Baron de Charlus, a gay megalomaniac who enjoys being whipped; Odette de Crécy, a courtesan who makes a smart marriage, and who has eyes so large they seem to droop beneath their own weight, putting the rest of her face under great strain; Charles Morel, a brutish opportunist who is also a brilliant player of the violin; and Charles Swann, a mysterious, cultured socialite who is also one of the most significant influences on the life of the narrator, Marcel. But, unlike a trip to the zoo or looking at a map, the experience of viewing these specimens is immensely time-consuming. It is not just that Proust's novel is long; it is also not the sort of long book with which one can make quick progress. His brother Robert commented that simply to have the time to read it you would need to be very ill or laid up with a broken leg. Delightfully, there is a Monty Python sketch, 'The All-England Summarize Proust Competition', in which contestants are required to explain *À la recherche* in fifteen seconds. One might just as soon lick one's elbow.

Proust's is a name to conjure with, but all this conjuring is evasive. It's a way of getting away from the fact that most people have very little idea of what his writing is about. The good news is that when you find yourself talking to another person about Proust, there is an excellent chance that you are both rather short of reliable information about what can be found between the covers of his books. The bad news is that people who actually have read Proust are adept at spotting the laxity that betrays a bullshitter. Then again, since *À la recherche* can be considered a case study of egotism, you can use it – use its name, the very fact of its existence – as a springboard to talk about yourself in a Proustian way, unpacking your life's baggage fluently.

'You know the interesting thing?' said a Scottish economist to whom I once chatted over lunch while on holiday in Egypt. 'Proust was a goalkeeper.' The interesting thing is that this is untrue. Proust was too frail to keep goal. The great literary goalkeeper was in fact Albert Camus, whose novel *The Outsider* has fuelled innumerable adolescent programmes of rebellion – and was the inspiration for several songs by a band who were essential when I was a teenager, The Cure. The song titles 'Boys Don't Cry', 'Killing an Arab': that's straight out of Camus. Typical of the nutty stuff you'd expect from a goal-keeper. And while we're about it, Camus, whose origins were among the working class of colonial Algeria, is an icon in France for political reasons (he was a moral opponent of the extremes of both communism and fascism), and beyond France because his name and his works call up thrilling images of defiant youth, individualism and the fiercest sort of existential angst.

But back to Marcel Proust. The things commonly known about *À la recherche* mean it is treated as being more than a little absurd. A tiny cake called a madeleine is dipped in tea and opens a flood of recollections: at the heart of these is the narrator's memory of how, lying in bed, he consoled himself with the thought that his mother would come up to his room and kiss him good night, but when she did eventually come he no longer really wanted her there. Anticipation is more pleasurable than achieving the thing anticipated. Another cogent idea here is that memories are involuntary; they are cued by sensory experiences that may seem to have only a weak connection with the actual content of what is being recalled. It is because of this that the unexpected triggering of memories is described as 'Proustian'. So, too, is a close examination of the enigmas of one's personal history; it is Proustian to journey, half dreamily, into the past and caress its details. Proustian, too, is a tendency to generalize – to say 'We think this' or 'We find that' – which has, I suppose, rubbed off on me.

Why is Proust sometimes treated as an almost laughable figure, and is he one?

Many people are aware that Proust's style is peculiar. His sentences are idiosyncratically long and digressive. They are often hard to follow. Here, chosen at random from Lydia Davis's translation of the first volume, is one sentence – take a deep breath! – from a description of a garden:

In another place one corner seemed reserved for the various common species, of a tidy white or pink like dame's-rocket, washed clean like porcelain with housewifely care, while a little farther off, others, pressed against one another in a true floating flower border, suggested garden pansies that had come like butterflies to rest their glossy blue-tinged wings on the transparent obliquity of that watery bed; of that celestial bed as well: for it gave the flowers a soil of a colour more precious, more affecting than the colour of the flowers themselves; and, whether it sparkled beneath the water-lilies in the afternoon in a kaleidoscope of silent, watchful and mobile contentment, or whether towards evening it filled, like some distant port, with the rose and reverie of the sunset, ceaselessly changing so as to remain in harmony, around the more fixed colours of the corollas themselves, with all that is most profound, most fleeting, most mysterious – all that is infinite – in the hour, it seemed to have made them flower in the middle of the sky itself.

That's 177 words of lyrical intensity: abundant yet also scientific. (One of Proust's sentences runs to 958 words.) Proust achieves the paradoxical effect of meandering purposefully. And this is something we can do. To be Proustian is to understand that what looks like a digression is often the real story, that no detail is too small to be worth notice (or comment), and that slowing down experience – or the *experience* of experience – is the most effective way of locating meaning amid the headlong rush of life. Proust offers what one could perhaps call density: the sense of entering the fourth dimension.

Proust himself is easily presented as an absurd figure, too: a nocturnal hypochondriac, frequently confined to his bed, keen on late-night rendezvous in expensive restaurants where he would typically leave a tip far larger than the bill, irritated by being described in a newspaper as a Jew (though he was one), inclined to keep on his overcoat and muffler at the dinner table, obsessive about the preparation of his coffee, enthusiastic about young men with moustaches, and dying after catching a cold.

At thirteen, and then a second time at twenty, Proust filled out a questionnaire of a sort popular among his social class. It ventured queries such as 'In what place would you like to live?' and 'For what faults do you have the greatest indulgence?' At thirteen, Proust answered the first of these questions, 'In the land of the Ideal, or rather of my ideal'. Seven years on, he recast this: 'In the place where certain things I want would come to pass as if by enchantment – and where tender feelings would always be shared'. This isn't exactly hearty pub fare, but Proust's questions include some that are highly relevant here. They are used each month in the back pages of *Vanity Fair* to coax thoughts from celebrities. The one that always strikes me is 'Who is your favourite hero of fiction?' Some surprising answers have been given, not least by writers. Norman Mailer chose Anna Karenina, Jay McInerney plumped for Stephen Dedalus, and Umberto Eco favoured Mickey Mouse. At least none of them said Proust's Marcel, a narcissist who regards other people as little more than the furnishings in life's apartment.

Why, though, would someone read Proust, this apparently absurd creator of absurdly serpentine sentences? One reason is that he is a satirical critic of snobbery, hypocrisy and disloyalty, and he approaches these and other vices ingeniously, showing us how pleasant they can be. Or rather, he brings to life some of the sensuous pleasure of being a bad person. Thus, for instance, lying, which is something we occasionally have to do in order to safeguard our pleasures, and which can spark off quite exquisite sensations. The tension between the rewards of being good and the rewards of being bad is carefully explored.

Proust is also, famously, profound in his treatment of memory. He explores the involuntary stirrings – as by a smell or a flavour – that bring to the surface a swell of forgotten images. Indeed, there may be no writer more psychologically acute, and he is not just a psychologist, but also a philosopher of that psychology. He writes at one point of how we lack a real understanding of our own 'visibility'. We imagine we are of great interest to people who in actual fact never give us a moment's thought, while there are others, whose interest we never suspect, to whom we are fascinating. I guess we like what Proust suggests about memory because it reassures us that nothing is ever quite lost to us. And, it would seem, he was prepared to lay down his life for his art.

Alain de Botton's *How Proust Can Change Your Life* (1997) identifies among the author's virtues his teaching us how to take our time and how to open our eyes to the beauty of simple things. Eating a slice of bread, for instance, can be far more pleasurable than eating a fancy dish such as ortolan – the little bird, that is, not the blue-skinned alien from *Star Wars*. De Botton suggests that Proust can help us stop wasting our lives and lead us to a more immediate appreciation of their preciousness. Suffering is helpful, because it provides a key to what is in truth 'the whole art of living'. Unhappiness can be productive, and value can be located in the most unexpected places.

Five ideas from Proust that may not change your life, but could help you make more of it

1. It's okay for your favourite subject to be yourself.
2. Truths about the past are elusive, but . . .
3. The past is never really over.
4. Avoid clichés.
5. Everything is connected.

The thing people never tell you about Proust – presumably because they don't know it – is that he is funny. There is received wisdom about authors, and much of it is spurious: one of my intentions here, if I have not already said as much, is to get you to kick against it. Proust, an author who is routinely cherished by people who have read no more than the title of his master-piece, seems to be one of those worst served by received wisdom. Even his admirers speak of him as gloomy. Yet he can be amusing in the way that your wicked neighbour at a wedding reception might be, pointing out the foibles and sartorial faux pas of the guests at other tables. For example, a party is an opportunity for a critique of the different styles of monocle worn by the guests. One man has a monocle which looks like a wound it might have been magnificent to receive; another's is tiny and requires a great deal of eye-clenching, with the droll effect of making women think he must be capable of suffering a great deal in love; a third, who has the big, round-eyed head of a carp, looks as if he has helpfully come to the party with a symbolic fragment of his aquarium; and yet another has a mon-ocle which makes his eye look like a specimen in a natural history museum, 'teeming with friendliness'. I haven't seen anyone wearing a monocle in over twenty years, but Proust makes me wish I had.

What does the title of Proust's novel mean, anyway?

Much more common than talk about Proust's sense of humour is a discussion of how he should be translated. Part of this debate concerns the best way to render his great novel's title in English. C. K. Scott-Moncrieff, Proust's first English translator, nabbed a line from a Shakespeare sonnet and dubbed it *Remembrance of Things Past*. A nice title, but inaccurate. *In Search of Lost Time* is now standard, but is much less felicitous, sounding more like an official report into ways of improving the network rail timetable. Arguments about which is preferable get to the heart of the problem of translation. There is no word-for-word correspondence between languages, so turning the French into English is not simply a mechanical procedure. In reality, translation is a competition between transparent expression and fidelity to the original, between a formal closeness to the source and a more dynamic approach that concerns itself with teasing out the essential meaning of a phrase. The opening sentence of *À la recherche*, a short one by Proust's standards, is 'Longtemps, je me suis couché de bonne heure.' This can be translated as 'For a long time, I went to bed early,' 'For ages, I have gone to bed early,' 'I used for a long time to go to bed early' and 'Time and again, I would go to bed early.' Which of these is best? When even the first sentence poses problems of this kind, you can be sure that talking about Proust's magnum opus offers large possibilities.

Differences of opinion about the craft of translation – differing views on the need for the translator to be invisible, for instance – present a significant problem for people who want to embrace literature generously. English literature is rich, but many of the greatest books have been written in other languages, and unless you are prodigiously polyglot – like, say, the eighteenth-century philologist Sir William Jones, who reportedly had a working knowledge of twenty-eight languages – you will find yourself relying on English versions. You might conceivably learn Italian so as to be able to read Dante in the original, or might learn it for other reasons and reap the wider benefit of having done so, but I doubt that an admirer – or someone who thinks she has the potential to be an admirer – of the fine contemporary novelist Harry Mulisch will learn Dutch in order to read him without the mediating and perhaps vitiating influence of his translators. The suspicion that this influence really is a negative one is pretty common, and it is with this in mind that I turn now to two authors whose works are vastly popular in translation – authors whom I for one do not expect ever to be able to read in the original, although I am certain much is lost when they are Englished.

11

WHY THE RUSSIANS? TOLSTOY AND DOSTOEVSKY

Lev Nikolayevich Tolstoy (1828–1910). Major works: *War and Peace, Anna Karenina*. His other writings include three autobiographical novels entitled *Childhood, Boyhood* and *Youth*, and a substantial work of moral philosophy, *The Kingdom of God Is Within You*.

Fyodor Mikhailovich Dostoevsky (1821–81). Major works: *Crime and Punishment, The Brothers Karamazov*. Another of his books, *Notes from Underground*, is sometimes described as an 'overture' heralding existentialist philosophy. For practical purposes, his name should be pronounced *doss-toh-yev-skee*.

Trivia: Tolstoy did not learn to ride a bicycle until he was sixty-seven years old. More sobering is the information that Dostoevsky, arrested in 1849 for being part of a group of liberal intellectuals, was subjected to a mock execution and sent before a firing squad – only to have his sentence commuted, to four years in a Siberian labour camp.

What is it about the Russian novel? We are taught, or at least encouraged, to venerate it. People who admire Russian literature speak of its sadness, a kind of soulful depth, the authors' special feel for the poetry of human relationships. Explaining the pleasures of reading Dostoevksy, Virginia Woolf described his books as 'seething whirlpools, gyrating sand-storms, waterspouts which hiss and boil and suck us in'. We are 'whirled round, blinded, suffocated, and at the same time filled with a giddy rapture'. Robert Louis Stevenson described *Crime and Punishment* as 'a house of life'; readers could venture inside it and be 'purified' while also being 'tortured'.

Tolstoy for his part is brilliantly realistic, a master of detail but also of the general. The fine contemporary critic James Wood has said that 'to be caught up in the bright sweep of Tolstoy's *War and Peace* . . . is to succumb to the contagion of vitality'. Tolstoy makes us feel alive: 'as his characters infect each other with the high temperature of their existence, so they infect us'. Henry James thought *War and Peace* a 'large loose baggy monster' (it's not so much one narrative as a network of narratives), and considered Tolstoy 'a monster harnessed to his great subject – all human life!'

The claim most often repeated is that these writers have an unparalleled ability to take us inside the minds of the characters they create; their mastery of psychology is profound, and they are especially interested in diseased, disordered, corrupt and wretched minds, which readers revel in inhabiting. Tolstoy seems in his books always to be on the move, and he takes us with him. Dostoevsky, meanwhile, is intense.

Yet there are plenty of things that make Russian novels offputting. To begin with, they tend to be long. More than a few people have been moved to wonder if the Russian day was somehow longer than ours is now. How did readers ever find the time for the half a million words of *War and Peace*, which in English translations tends to run to about 1,300 pages? They must have had a lot of servants. Then you have the names, complete with patronymics (and often with diminutives). We can deal with characters who have simple names – Pip, Tom and Emma – or at least manageable ones – Dorothea, Gudrun – but not with characters who are called (repeatedly) Nastasya Filippovna, Lizaveta Prokofyevna, Varvara Ardaliovna and Natalia Nikitishna, as in Dostoevsky's *The Idiot*. Can you keep track of who all these people are? Perhaps. But each time such a name appears on the page, its many syllables put a brake on the fluency of one's reading.

Moreover, for Russian writers of the nineteenth century, the novel was a vehicle for intellectual debate, and many of their works are steeped in contemporary ideas about metaphysics, the influence of the Swiss philosopher Jean-Jacques Rousseau, a fascination with the supernatural, the myths of Russian Orthodoxy, and even a cult of Napoleon. Finally, translations of Russian novels can be execrable, and those that are good are still uncomfortable. Tolstoy's deliberate repetitions have been avoided by some translators, who prefer a little elegant variation; when the repetitions are rendered, they can grate. Virginia Woolf observed that, in forming their view of the classic Russian novelists, most readers 'have judged a whole literature stripped of its style'. 'Thus treated', she thought, these writers are 'like men deprived by an earthquake or a railway accident not only of all their clothes, but also of something subtler and more important – their manners, the idiosyncrasies of their characters'.

Tolstoy and Dostoevsky are often paired – but why?

While the two of them wrote at the same time and in the same language, is this enough of a link? It is most useful, I'd suggest, to contrast them. Among the main differences are the way Tolstoy stretches time, whereas Dostoevsky zeroes in on the throb of particular moments; Tolstoy writes mainly about people who could easily be considered normal, whereas Dostoevsky deals in more extreme personalities; and Tolstoy is a moralist who wishes also to be a teacher, whereas Dostoevsky possesses much less moral certainty.

The philosopher Isaiah Berlin wrote a book about Tolstoy entitled *The Hedgehog and the Fox*. The inspiration for the title was the Greek poet Archilocus, who suggested that 'The fox knows many things, but the hedgehog knows one big thing.' To paraphrase: there are those among us who relate everything to a central, defining vision or principle, and there are those who pursue many different goals and whose thoughts are scattered. Tolstoy is, according to Berlin, 'by nature a fox', but he 'believed in being a hedgehog'. What makes him a hedgehog is a philosophy which can be summed up as follows: individual people experience something they believe to be free will and choice, but in their relationships with others they are governed by the inexorable forces of history.

Berlin's idea is suggestive, because we can classify everyone as either a hedgehog or a fox. He considered Dostoevsky a hedgehog – a position that just about holds up. Dostoevsky is a fine storyteller, albeit one whose plots sometimes rely too much on coincidence, and he is an experimental writer of real originality, but his greatest gift is for character. His novels are full of magnificently dysfunctional individuals. The condition was one he knew well. When he was a trainee engineer, he apparently designed a very fine fortress, which nevertheless had a glaring fault – it lacked both windows and doors. Later, he pawned his ailing wife's warmest coat so that he could go off gambling, and also pawned his wife's earrings and his wedding ring. His pursuit of the thrill of a bet was feverish, and he shares with his characters a knowledge of what it is to stand on the precipice looking into the abyss of ruin. In the words of the novelist David Foster Wallace, Dostoevsky wrote about 'the stuff that's really important', namely death and morality, identity, the different kinds of love, freedom, our powers of reason and faith, obsession and the force of the human will. He engages deeply with these concerns; the depth of his engagement is almost embarrassing to the modern reader. 'And', as Wallace points out, 'he did it without ever reducing his characters to mouthpieces or his books to tracts.'

Dostoevsky's best-known book is *Crime and Punishment*, which is set in a dirty, decadent and stifling St Petersburg. The main character, Raskolnikov, is a penniless and self-absorbed student who hatches a plan to kill an old woman, a widely disliked pawnbroker. (His name comes from *raskolnik*, 'a dissenter'. In Dostoevsky's novels the symbolism of names is undeniably heavy.) He executes the crime – also having to kill the pawnbroker's sister – and in its aftermath grows increasingly paranoid, believing that everyone suspects him. In this he is not unlike Shakespeare's Macbeth, fearful and haunted. One early reviewer, Lafcadio Hearn, warned his audience that reading the book might make them ill.

Raskolnikov's justification for what he has done is that the murder, while plainly hateful, removes from the world someone no better than a louse, and ultimately it will allow him to do good. Additionally, it enables him to assert his freedom. He believes he has the mental strength to live with his crime; he likens himself to Napoleon, a figure set above the rest of society by being self-made and decisive. But did these thoughts precede the crime, or are they present only as he looks back on it? Dostoevsky wrote in his notebook that Raskolnikov's 'moral development begins with the crime itself'. You could in fact say that *Crime and Punishment* is a back-to-front novel: the crime comes first, and the consideration of the crime comes afterwards.

Crime and Punishment and Dostoevsky's later (final) masterpiece, *The Brothers Karamazov*, are alike in one key respect: they place the reader inside the mind of a criminal. In *Crime and Punishment* we share in the enormity of Raskolnikov's despicable act. His experience is the book's centre. In *The Brothers Karamazov* we again see the workings of strange psychologies, although in this case our perspective is more that of an outsider looking in. At the very outset we gather that the novel is a murder story – the opening sentence refers to Fyodor Karamazov's 'gloomy and tragic death' – and the focus is on who is responsible. Both novels have evasive, tricksy narrators. Instead of projecting one clear voice, the books resound with voices. In *Crime and Punishment* the narrator drops in and out of the telling; he is embroiled in the drama of events, but then steps back from it, saying for instance, 'I shall not describe what took place,' or claiming that the imagery of some dreams is so artistically perfect that 'no person awake, including the dreamer himself, even if he were an artist like Pushkin or Turgenev, could imagine them'. The effect is disorientating. For its part *The Brothers Karamazov* can be considered 'polyphonic'; each of the major characters has a distinctive voice which is at certain points audible in the story's telling. Moreover, the narrator seems to speak with two different voices: as a local resident familiar with the Karamazovs, and as the author himself.

Dostoevsky completed his last novel only a couple of months before his death. Fyodor Karamazov, an energetic monster of a man, has three sons: one debauched, one intellectual, and one a visionary. In addition, his cook Pavel Smerdyakov (whose name has connotations of both churlishness and foul smell) is rumoured to be his illegitimate child, fathered on a mute girl who wanders the streets. From the title onwards, the novel invites the question 'How many brothers are there?' All are spiritual creatures, preoccupied with the punishment that awaits them in the afterlife. Dmitri, also known as Mitya, is the eldest, the only child of Karamazov's first marriage. He loves women, drink and entertainment, and is useless with money. The youngest legitimate son, Alyosha, has little understanding of earthly passions; he is a godly sort, who resides in a monastery and dreams of harmony among his fellow men. (Rather wonderfully, in MGM's 1958 film of the novel this strange youth was played by William Shatner.) Most interesting of the three is the middle son Ivan, often called Vanya, a trained mathematician who finds the world absurd, is racked by doubt, rebels against God and has an interview with an imaginary devil who mocks his powers of reason. The epileptic Smerdyakov, for his part, is the classic damaged child. He haunts the brothers, and is their distorted double, a lackey who is also a parody of their different weaknesses. Transfixed by Dostoevsky's picture of darkly intertwined relationships, Freud thought *Karamazov* the best of all novels, and was particularly intrigued by the possibility that the author's neurotic relationship to his father, who died when he was eighteen, fed the book's scenes of family discord.

The novel is a broad one, big and elaborate, but its most celebrated episode is concentrated in a single chapter, 'The Grand Inquisitor', which occurs about a third of the way through. Ivan and Alyosha are sitting in a stinking tavern, and Ivan tells a story about Christ returning to earth – Seville, in fact – at the time of the Spanish Inquisition. Christ is intent on reinforcing his previous teachings, and the people are thrilled to see him, especially when he raises a little girl from the dead. But he is thrown in jail and sentenced to death because, as the Grand Inquisitor explains, his presence is certain to interfere with the work of the Catholic Church. Christ listens silently to the Grand Inquisitor's words, and at length kisses him on the lips. Then he departs. The ambiguous confrontation between Christ and the Inquisitor is really a confrontation within Ivan, between the essentially Catholic mission to achieve communal happiness (which involves giving up one's freedom and submitting to the sort of totalitarian values that define the Inquisition) and the Protestant desire for freedom without unity (which, by allowing individuals to take responsibility for themselves, puts them at risk of misery). Memorably odd though it may be, the story is a bit corny; its rhetoric is deliberately over the top, and its real interest lies in the way it shows that Ivan, tormented by his concern about God's absence from the world, is in the thrall of something demonic.

Dostoevsky has a great deal to say about demonic creatures – one of his novels even has the title *The Devils* – and he makes a connection between artistry and devilry. In part this has to do with his Christian concerns about the hereafter: in part it has to do with the idea that creativity is a Faustian pact. Telling stories is never far away from telling lies. One of the characters

---

Six other Russian novelists (because there are plenty of others, many of them brilliant)

1. Ivan Goncharov, author of *Oblomov*, a novel about a sensitive young man of quite incredible inertia.

2. Mikhail Bulgakov. His best-known novel is *The Master and Margarita*, supposedly the inspiration for the Rolling Stones' song 'Sympathy for the Devil'.

3. Alexander Solzhenitsyn, legendary for his exposé of the Soviet labour camps.

4. Andrei Bely. Known chiefly for *Petersburg*, a novel about a revolutionary who is required to murder his father. *Petersburg* is sometimes for structural and linguistic reasons likened to Joyce's *Ulysses*.

5. Nikolai Gogol. His *Dead Souls* centres on Chichikov, an ambitious scoundrel who tries to acquire social standing by buying up the 'souls' of dead serfs whose owners still have to pay poll-tax on them.

6. Ivan Turgenev (pronounced *toor-gay-nyeff*, with the stress on the middle syllable). In his masterpiece, *Fathers and Sons*, the character Yevgeny Bazarov is a nihilist who rejects the familiar values of society – an angry young man drawn with great skill.

---

in *The Devils*, Stepan Trofimovich, says that 'real truth is never true-to-life', and 'in order to make the truth true-to-life you really have to stir a bit of falsehood into it'. Life, it seems, cannot avoid being polluted.

How is Tolstoy different, then?

While Dostoevsky's novels are full of society, they are essentially personal dramas about freedom and conscience. Tolstoy operates on a grander scale. *War and Peace* is a national epic, a picture of history as what Tolstoy calls 'the unconscious swarmlike life of mankind'. It is also a paean to the significance of things typically seen as trifling: the way someone holds a cigar to keep it from getting dirty with blood on the battlefield, or a character's missing the delicious effect of his planting a farewell kiss on his sister's forehead because he is staring into the darkness of an open door. More straightforwardly, it is the story of the dignified Bolkonskys, tucked away on their old-fashioned country estate, the Rostovs, a family of spirited Moscow aristocrats, and Pierre Bezukhov, a generous, emotional misfit whose name literally translates as 'Peter Earless', and whose fortunes are enmeshed with those of both families. It contains more than 500 characters, many of whom are deftly realized but then evaporate, and is full of plotlines that are set up, then seemingly abandoned.

Here I find myself thinking of the Woody Allen gag: 'I took a speed-reading course and read *War and Peace* in twenty minutes. It involves Russia.' It does, of course, but what survives in the memory is something else. Memories of books are fragmentary, not complete. What I recall will differ from what someone else recalls. For me *War and Peace* means Pierre. Pierre, who has hardly any idea how to enter a drawing room and still less idea how to leave one, pulling at the plume of a hat belonging to a general which he has mistaken for his own. Pierre talking to a soldier who, like him, has been imprisoned in a ruined church, and eating with relish a potato the soldier has been keeping wrapped up in a rag. Pierre with his bearskin coat flung open, being driven on his sleigh through the Moscow night, and seeing a comet curiously fixed among the stars like an arrow stuck in the ground. Pierre, drunkenly pacing in his room at his father's house, threatening the wall as though thrusting a rapier at an invisible enemy, glowering all the while over the rims of his spectacles, and imagining he is Napoleon, has just captured London and is dealing with the 'traitor' William Pitt. Yet the most remarkable moment in the novel, for me, occurs when Pierre's high-minded friend Prince Andrei Bolkonsky is listening to his wife in labour; he is in the next-door room, and amid the sounds of her dying he makes out a baby's cry. 'What have they taken a baby in there for?' he wonders. Only after an instant's bewilderment does he realize that the baby is his.

Anna Karenina is a more compact novel – still very long, but not oceanic. It opens with the twin statements 'All happy families are alike. Each unhappy family is unhappy in its own way.' The claims are seductive – and untrue. We are being invited to challenge them. But the opening immediately points to the book's main concern: the idea of family. Furthermore, it creates a philosophical framework for the story. Tolstoy is emphasizing that he is not just a storyteller. The novel's celebrated epigraph, 'Vengeance is mine; I will repay,' is taken from St Paul's Epistle to the Romans in the New Testament, which itself refers to the Old Testament book of Deuteronomy. Asked what this was all about, Tolstoy said he meant to 'explain the idea that the bad things people do have as their consequence all the bitter things, which come not from people, but from God'. The epigraph signals Tolstoy's concern in the novel not with vengeance, but with the whole spectrum of moral values and judgements.

The very fundamentals of the plot make it clear that in *Anna Karenina* the lives, values and commitments of the characters are desperately tangled. At the start of the novel we find out that Stiva, otherwise known as Oblonsky, has been unfaithful to his wife Dolly with their children's French governess. He asks his sister Anna to persuade Dolly not to leave him. Meanwhile, Stiva's old friend Levin, otherwise known as Kostya, offers to marry Dolly's sister, Kitty. But Kitty believes she will receive an offer of marriage from Vronsky, a cavalry officer. Vronsky has no such offer in mind. Yet, as we see, he is susceptible to the charms of Anna.

For Tolstoy, marriage is a social contract, and those who violate it can expect to be the victims of tragedy. Anna is married to Karenin, a respected government official. She is much admired, but feels dissatisfied, living as she does in her husband's shadow. On a trip to Moscow she briefly encounters the handsome and cultivated Vronsky. He is struck by the friendly attention she pays him, and by her mixture of decisiveness and grace. Soon after, they meet again. Their attraction is wild. It is hardly giving the game away to say that eventually they come together in a blaze of passion. Gradually, others sense that Anna and

Vronsky are having an affair. The rest I can leave to your imagination. Just think, like Proust's narrator, of that familiar sensation of wanting something above all else, craving it endlessly, believing it will never truly be yours, and then eventually getting it, and, the moment you properly possess it, being disappointed and bored. As Tolstoy has Vronsky recognize, receiving what you long for provides 'only one grain of the mountain of bliss . . . anticipated'. One of people's cardinal mistakes lies in 'imagining that happiness consists in the gratification of their wishes'.

Again, detail is crucial to Tolstoy's revelation of the complexity and uncanniness of emotions. For instance, after taking the night train home to St Petersburg, Anna is startled by the sight of her waiting husband's ears. 'Why do his ears look like that?' she asks herself, noticing the way they seem to prop up the brim of his round hat. He looks at her wearily, and her heart is gripped by an unpleasant sensation; she is unhappy with her reaction to seeing him, and perhaps also with him for not prompting a warmer reaction.

The most famous scene in the novel occurs when Levin decides to mow a field on his estate. The scene expresses beautifully what in sport is known as being 'in the zone'. After a time, Levin finds that the work becomes pleasant and straightforward. As he cuts the grass, he barely notices what he is doing; he feels light and free, and his cutting is crisp. But when he recalls what he is doing the work becomes difficult again and his cutting is less skilful. So it is with sport – and perhaps also with other things, such as writing or having sex. When you think too closely about what you are doing, it is effortful and lacklustre, but when you slip into a pleasurable unconsciousness, a kind of automatic performance, the act seems to take care of itself. This is bliss: an easy excellence, which feels as though it happens outside time and space. It is also, incidentally, why elite sportspeople tend to be uninteresting on the subject of their art; at its most sublime moments, they are hardly conscious of how it is achieved. Here, in just such a sublime moment, Levin lives fully in the present, and he is open to sensations he has never before imagined. His workers' bread and the kvass they drink taste exquisite, and he feels closer to the people who work his land than he does to members of his own family. The land itself looks new. He does not feel tired. It is as though he has been driven forward by a force that exists outside him. This is what it feels like to live in the real.

The mowing scene, which spans two chapters, is so freshly realistic a depiction of experiences that we feel we can touch and taste what Levin touches and tastes. The scene highlights Levin's distance from the peasant class. In temporarily feeling close to them, he betrays the real extent of his remoteness from them. The idyllic impression of togetherness is fleeting. But Levin learns from what he sees and feels. When he returns home, he understands just how limited his relationship with his half-brother Sergey is, and how limited Sergey's philanthropy is. Levin has experienced a genuine closeness, a richer kind of communication, whereas Sergey, though concerned in his way with the public good, seems too fixated with theories. Sergey is an example of a particular type in whom Tolstoy is interested, the 'counterfeit thinker' whose understanding of the world derives not from observation, but from an impractical scheme of ideas. By contrast, Levin is free from pretence. His experience in the mowing scene shapes his sense that to be truly vital is to be empty of all the things with which one has so assiduously and tediously filled up the open spaces of one's existence.

The mowing episode combines Tolstoy's ability to evoke and delight in the phenomena of everyday life with the political aspect of his writing. He is a great writer because of his ability to fuse the epic and the intimate; he is psychologically perceptive – alive to the tiny details of behaviour – and at the same time sees the grand sweep of history. *War and Peace*, frequently acclaimed as the greatest novel ever written, is a book of strange simplicity; it is dense, it is interspersed with historical essays, and, as I have mentioned, some of its plotlines peter out mysteriously, but the experience of reading it is so satisfyingly immediate that none of its difficulties seems formidable. To taste Tolstoy's novel is indeed to be swept along by it.

Tolstoy is the biggest of the Russian novelists – a faintly embarrassing thing to say – because his books seem so densely peopled, so generous in their capacity to encompass human experience, so psychologically acute amid their giant unfoldings. He is rare among the authors of long novels in leaving one wishing his books were longer. Rare, too, in that the immense labour he expended on his art is something of which we are barely conscious as we devour it.

How to damn a writer with praise

Damning something with faint praise is familiar to all of us: 'This potato salad is not objectionable,' 'Her dress went really well with her eye shadow.' Sometimes, though, it is possible to damn with rather greater praise. For instance,

Turgenev gained a curious sort of revenge on Tolstoy, with whom he had quarrelled, by pronouncing him 'a real giant among the rest of our literary brothers' and then declaring that his works produced 'the impression of an elephant in a show: ungainly, even absurd – but enormous'. The notion that Tolstoy is an elephantine writer has dogged his reputation ever since.

For those looking to emulate Turgenev, the usual formula is to make an exceptionally large claim ('Don DeLillo may well be our greatest living writer') and then slyly undercut it ('He has the knack of converting an ordinary descriptive sentence into an unusual aphorism'). Damning with praise – be it faint or fulsome – is a favourite trick of book reviewers: 'This is undoubtedly the best novel yet written about village life in fifteenth-century Flanders.'

12

WHY DO PEOPLE KEEP ON ABOUT THE NINETEENTH-CENTURY NOVEL?

The nineteenth century was a fertile period for fiction. Its stars included not just Tolstoy and Dostoevsky, but also the French writers Gustave Flaubert, Honoré de Balzac, Stendhal and Emile Zola, as well as the Portuguese realist Eça de Queirós.

The major English-language figures included Charles Dickens, George Eliot, the Brontë sisters (Charlotte, Emily and Anne), Thomas Hardy, Elizabeth Gaskell, Sir Walter Scott, Herman Melville and Henry James.

When Tolstoy surveyed the literature of his age, he considered Charles Dickens its greatest figure, and it was under Dickens's influence that the Russian wrote his auto-biographical *Childhood*. But Dickens and Tolstoy are vastly different writers. Articulating this with his customary clarity, George Orwell argued that the two men's artistic purposes 'barely intersect'. An admirer of Dickens, Orwell could nonetheless believe that he was unintelligible outside the English-speaking world – and perhaps even to certain groups within it. Tolstoy, by contrast, had a near-universal appeal. 'Tolstoy's characters can cross a frontier,' he wrote. 'Dickens's can be portrayed on a cigarette-card.' 'Tolstoy's grasp seems to be so much larger,' he concluded. The grasp he had in mind was Tolstoy's comprehension of history. But, he insisted, this did not make Dickens inferior, and 'one is no more obliged to choose between them than between a sausage and a rose'.

For a modern perspective on the essential qualities of Dickens, we might turn to the BBC's *Bleak House*, one of the cultural events of 2005. It was screened in half-hour episodes – shorter than usual for a period drama – in a move designed to make it attractive to an audience more used to the nuggety instalments of *EastEnders*. The gambit was far from being cheeky, as many Victorian novels were published as serials; their readers, like the audience for modern soaps, were tantalized by cliff-hangers and waited impatiently for their next dose of excitement. While Dickens was not the first writer to publish his work serially, he was the first who intended his publications in this form to be more than merely short-lived squibs. The profitable but inflexible nature of the form had consequences for his art: typically, Dickens's novels have large casts of characters, most of whom have mannerisms designed to make them memorable, and his plots are episodic and full of incident. While numerous other writers experienced the pressures of serial publication, Dickens was remarkable in the way he built on the rapport it created by giving public readings. These readings, hugely successful, made Dickens a Victorian forerunner of the modern preachers, comedians and pop acts who fill concert halls and football stadiums.

Dickens was a populist, and his novels are grounded in a world that his public would have recognized. Rather than being one of those writers who exults in being far from home, he lavishes attention on the mundane. Ordinary things are made fabulous – or sinister. There is a lot, for instance, about food; how much people consume, and what they consume, is a key to their moral worth as well as to their social status. (This is good dinner-party fare: the meaning of what we eat.) The city is Dickens's terrain, and that means above all London, a place both repellent to him and infinitely desirable, a scene of personal humiliations – notably, his period as a twelve-year-old spent working at Warren's Blacking Factory – yet also of inexhaustible possibilities. It is both modern and medieval, a hive and a wilderness. On the opening page of *Bleak House*, London's November streets are so choked with mud that 'it would not be wonderful to meet a Megalosaurus, forty feet long or so, waddling like an elephantine lizard up Holborn Hill'. It is also a place of commercial rather than industrial activity, and its energy vibrates through his energetic prose.

Dickens excels in creating memorable characters: grown-up children and childlike grown-ups, frosty spinsters, cheery incompetents, exhausted wives, threadbare ruined men and crabbed little villains. He animates them using a wealth of detail. Actually, many are not so much animated by detail as trapped inside it. In *Our Mutual Friend*, one of Dickens's more underrated novels, there is a schoolmistress, Miss Peecher, who is described as 'a little pincushion, a little housewife, a little book, a little workbox, a little set of tables and weights and measures, and a little woman, all in one'. The repetition of 'little' is diversionary; what we are meant to see – but not too quickly – is that she is neat, and that her neatness is a kind of stiffness, an absence of vitality. In the same novel there is another female character who is a 'species of lobster – throwing off a shell every forenoon, and needing to keep into a retired spot until the new crust hardens'. We know immediately what she is like. The surreal and the perverted are never far away in Dickens. Everything has its shadow.

Solid specifics are Dickens's forte. Mr Gradgrind, the fact-obsessed schoolmaster in *Hard Times*, is forever 'staggering over the universe with his rusty stiff-legged compasses'. The very tie around his neck has been 'trained to take him by the throat with an unaccommodating grasp, like a stubborn fact'. Miss Murdstone in *David Copperfield* has a hard steel purse, which she keeps in a bag that 'shut up like a bite'. Captain Cuttle in *Dombey and Son* is 'one of those timber-looking men, suits of oak as well as hearts'. Daniel Quilp, the deformed villain of *The Old Curiosity Shop*, eats prawns with the heads and tails still on, and when he has a hard-boiled egg consumes the shell. In case we don't get the message, we are told as well that he keeps an effigy of a sailor in his room, and likes nothing more than to spear it with a red-hot poker.

Partly because of his exaggerations and theatrical exuberance, Dickens was once dismissed as a mere 'entertainer', lacking seriousness. Many people still find it hard to see the point of him. His characters are condemned for being too persistently comic. His plots are seen as flabby, sentimental and ludicrous – a consequence, perhaps, of his books' publication as part-works. His style of writing is considered at times excessively ornate. Another, rather different sort of objection, perceived by Orwell, is that he is too English. Those who dismiss him, though, seem immune to humour, and have failed to discern that humour is truth speeded up.

How do Dickens's contemporaries compare with him?

Radically different from Dickens is the world of George Eliot. Where Dickens is melodramatic and an entertainer, Eliot is coolly analytical; Eliot has a philosophy of existence – and a solemn one at that – where Dickens has none; and whereas Dickens skews the reader's understanding of the everyday world, encouraging one to see it from a different angle, Eliot shows normality in its familiar colours, and brings to bear on it a refined moral and aesthetic intelligence. If you didn't know it before, you'll know by now that George Eliot was a woman – her real name was Mary Ann Evans – but the fact should be reiterated to stave off future embarrassment. Other women have written as men (the Brontë sisters Charlotte, Emily and Anne as Currer, Ellis and Acton Bell; Aurore Dudevant as George Sand; Karen Blixen as Isak Dinesen) and some have carefully used gender-unspecific names, such as S. E. Hinton and J. K. Rowling. Mary Ann Evans became George Eliot to escape the condescension so often heaped on female authors by Victorian reviewers, and also to preserve her privacy – a pressing need, as her decision to live with George Henry Lewes, a married man, would have struck most of her contemporaries as scandalous. I suspect there have been many people who, knowing she's a woman, imagine she was called Georgina. What is for certain is that if you make the mistake of thinking this George was a man, you'll be treated with sneery hauteur.

Eliot wrote seven novels, but her reputation rests chiefly on one, *Middlemarch*, which is frequently held up as the finest example of Victorian fiction. The novel's subtitle is 'A Study of Provincial Life'. Its setting is a provincial town around 1830, where the main business seems to be the manufacture of silk ribbons, but its style is sophisticated – reflecting that cultural gap between 1830 and the time when it was written, forty years later. In fact, it is a study of two marriages in their infancy. Where an Austen novel might finish, with bride and groom heading off into the bower of bliss, *Middlemarch* picks up.

Virginia Woolf considered *Middlemarch* one of the few English novels 'written for grown-up people'. What did she mean? Woolf was intent on rescuing Eliot from neglect, and what she admired was Eliot's psychological acuity. One of the novel's main concerns is the relationship between Dorothea Brooke, an energetic and intellectually curious heiress, and Edward Casaubon, a dry, inactive cleric who is absorbed in writing a 'Key to All Mythologies'. They marry, and it is not a happy union. Dorothea chooses at first to overlook Casaubon's faults – the hairy moles on his face, his mind's being in his own words 'something like the ghost of an ancient' – but soon she sees her mistake, reflecting that 'it is very difficult to be learned; it seems as if people were worn out on the way to great thoughts'. The couple's honeymoon in Rome is a disaster. In an especially disturbing moment Celia, Dorothea's sister, is described as 'regarding Mr Casaubon's learning as a kind of damp which might in due time saturate a neighbouring body'. This damp, seeping into a neighbouring body – Dorothea's

Five miserable moments in Victorian novels

1. In Thomas Hardy's *Jude the Obscure*, Jude's precocious child Little Father Time, aware of his family's financial difficulties, kills his half-siblings and then himself, leaving a note that reads 'Done because we are too menny'.

2. The failure of Mr Tulliver's lawsuit in George Eliot's *The Mill on the Floss*, which results in ruin for his family. 'They had gone forth together into their life of sorrow,' the narrator explains, referring to his children Tom and Maggie, before memorably rubbing in the point: 'They had entered the thorny wilderness, and the golden gates of their childhood had forever closed behind them.'

3. Towards the end of *Wuthering Heights*, Nelly Dean sees Heathcliff dead, lying on his back and appearing to smile. She tries to close his eyes – 'to extinguish, if possible, that frightful, life-like gaze of exultation' – but cannot. 'They would not shut: they seemed to sneer at my attempts; and his parted lips and sharp white teeth sneered too!'

4. The sentimentally imagined death of Little Nell in Dickens's *The Old Curiosity Shop*. Oscar Wilde said, 'One would have to have a heart of stone to read the death of Little Nell without laughing.'

5. In Charles Kingsley's *The Water Babies*, Tom the ten-year-old chimney-sweep is found in a little girl's room and flees in a panic. Eventually, he dies, is transformed into a 'water baby' and receives a moral re-education, but it is the build-up to this that is laden with pathos. Especially pathetic is the moment when Kingsley describes him crawling down a slope as if down a chimney – 'and so on, till – oh dear me! I wish it was all over; and so did he'.

body – is the perfect image with which to sum up Dorothea's sexual misery. It is revolting, yet quietly so.

There is plenty to say about the period's many other novelists, but a few brisk sketches will have to do. Elizabeth Gaskell was a subtle analyst of relationships and communities (as in *Cranford* and *Wives and Daughters*), yet also a voice of social protest (notably in *North and South* and *Mary Barton*). Thomas Hardy is often thought of as presenting the rural world idyllically, but his tragic novels, for all their dense pastoral tableaux, in fact present the disharmonies of rural living – and are full of characters competing with each other viciously, for sex and money and opportunity. Anthony Trollope, who is credited with introducing the pillar-box into Britain, produced forty-seven novels that manage to be both utterly mundane in their settings and brilliant in suggesting the shifting terrain of Victorian politics. It was Trollope who declared William Makepeace Thackeray the preeminent author of the age, which seems baffling to a modern audience, familiar perhaps only with the vivid sprawl of *Vanity Fair*. Thackeray was humorous and irreverent, but today comes across as too intrusive a presence in his books. Dickens's friend Wilkie Collins wrote suspenseful detective novels that are also sensitive to the violence of domestic life.

The Brontë sisters are grouped together for obvious reasons, yet are very different. Charlotte, the eldest and her parents' third child, wrote four novels, of which the best is *Jane Eyre*. Her books depict rebellious and lonely women struggling to achieve independence. Emily is known for a single book, *Wuthering Heights*, which, unlike Charlotte's novels, attracted almost universal hostility from the contemporary reading public. A violent and passionate domestic love story, it is famous above all for the character of Heathcliff, a savage, brooding and destructive orphan who is consumed by desire for his foster sister Catherine. Anne, the last of the six Brontë children to be born and reputedly the most attractive of the three, wrote two novels, *Agnes Grey* and *The Tenant of Wildfell Hall*, that engaged very obviously with the drug-taking of her brother Branwell, suggesting the vulnerability of women in the face of debauched male habits and the corruption of a society still bossed by men.

Wuthering Heights has many similarities to a book published a few years later which, on the face of it, promises to be radically different: Herman Melville's *Moby-Dick*. Both are boldly unChristian. Both, too, are set in remote places; their heroes are vengeful and damaged, slaves to guilt and the lure of evil. Both are narrated by people whose ordinariness makes them seem very different from the chief characters. The connection is unexpected, but the art of making literary connections involves surprise. *King Lear* is like Dante's *Paradiso*. *The Lion King* resembles *Hamlet*. Proust appears steeped in Freud – or is it the other way round?

Moby-Dick begins arrestingly: 'Call me Ishmael.' The invitation is ripe with a Biblical-sounding promise. Ishmael is a sailor, formerly a teacher, who wants to see the world. He travels aboard the *Pequod*, a venerable, noble, melancholy-seeming whaling ship commanded by Captain Ahab. Ishmael records the history of the *Pequod*'s voyage. Usually whaling crews seize on whatever opportunities come their way, but the *Pequod*'s mission is different. Ahab, described by one of his crew as 'a grand, ungodly, god-like man' and distinctly reminiscent of Heathcliff, is determined to revenge himself on the fierce white whale that on a previous trip trashed his boat and bit off his leg – a leg that was, as another sailor puts it, 'devoured, chewed up, crunched' by this monstrous creature. This is Ahab's obsession: he has an all-consuming need to find and kill his whale, no matter what the cost. His quest is a picture of tyranny. Melville wrote, on finishing the novel, 'I have written a wicked book and feel spotless as a lamb.' This may seem bizarre, but Melville knew he risked outrage by offering so sumptuous a portrait of a quest as dark and destructive as Ahab's, and believed he could justify his decision to create such a hate-filled and fanatical character because the grand manner in which he wrote about him was so bold and original. *Moby-Dick* is perhaps the classic example of a story which engrosses not despite the unpleasantness and narcissism of its main character, but because of them – and thanks to its author's charisma as a storyteller.

Nothing in the novel stands out more sharply, however, than those opening words. 'Call me Ishmael': the rhetorical gesture is one we recognize. Someone insists we call him by a particular name – often this is a wholly innocent move, yet then there are the people who make a fuss about being called something we might not otherwise think to call them. In a novel of the same time but a very different setting, Flaubert's *Madame Bovary*, we see this clearly. The 'Madame' of the title is important, for this is how Emma Bovary demands to be known. Meanwhile, her husband Charles is called 'Doctor' by characters keen to endear themselves to him. (He isn't actually a proper doctor, but rather a fumbling medical officer, so is flattered by the title. He's also no reader, having failed to slice open the uncut pages of his medical dictionary.) The men who call him *docteur* are manoeuvring skilfully. By charming him, they make it easier to cosy up to his alluring wife.

This novel of adultery is Flaubert's acknowledged master-piece. The subject was so common in nineteenth-century fiction that the poet Charles Baudelaire, reviewing *Madame Bovary*, called it 'the most worn out, prostituted theme of all, the tiredest of barrel organs'. The familiarity of the theme did not prevent *Madame Bovary* from being prosecuted for obscenity – something it has in common with *Ulysses*, *Lady Chatterley's Lover*, Radclyffe Hall's lesbian novel *The Well of Loneliness* and Baudelaire's own *Les Fleurs du mal*.

For Flaubert (pronounced *flow-bear*, with the emphasis on *flow*), adultery was something beautiful. Emma Bovary is a remarkable heroine for a nineteenth-century novel in being so very far from exemplary. Throughout, she is a work of art; her deceptions are awful, but they are to be cherished. Sometimes Flaubert goes too far. Emma's delicately laced corset, for instance, is said to slither from her hips with a snake's hiss. But usually his details are perfectly achieved, like those of a master painter. The impact of his writing is relentlessly visual. His style can be harmonious, but it can also be calculatedly awkward. For him sentences are, as he chose to put it, adventures. A character's living quarters are described, and we are shown, cinematically, eight mahogany chairs, a clock in the shape of a temple, and a barometer hanging on the wall. Another is shown by a shopkeeper a selection of his wares, which includes four egg-cups that have been carefully carved from coconut-shells by convicts. In his diary the author records a visit to a Turkish whore, mentioning that 'Her little dog slept on my silk jacket on the divan.' Flaubert constantly affords us impressions. We see what his characters see. If you're feeling brave, you could even say that Flaubert revolutionized the use in literature of the imperfect tense: English translations render this as 'She was going' or 'She used to go', but in the original French the two senses are not distinguished. Events are presented as part of a sort of flow, and the effect is to allow the reader to live the action of the novel almost as if in the present.

When Charles Bovary goes to dine with Emma and her father, before he and Emma are married, we hear little of the conversation that passes between them, but we share Charles's impression of Emma: her neck rises from a turned-down white collar, and her hair has been brushed so that it seems to be a single piece, and its black folds reveal just the very tip of her ear, while at her temples it is wavy. This isn't just a description of Emma; this is Charles appraising her, sizing her up, enjoying her appearance. And other characters do the same thing. Rodolphe Boulanger, the practised womanizer who thinks he can impress her by wearing long soft boots, looks at her out of the corner of his eye as they walk down the street, and 'on voyait entre ses lèvres le bout nacré de ses dents blanches' – one could see between her lips the pearly tips of her white teeth. This 'one' is Rodolphe, but also the reader; we are being made complicit in Rodolphe's fascination. Proust suggested that reading him was like being on board a moving pavement – a prototype of the travelators we ride at the airport, you could say – and watching a procession of images go by. What characters see tells us about their powers of judgement, too. Charles Bovary is impressed by Emma's perfectly white fingernails, which he thinks are a mark of elegance. We may think that, as a farmer's daughter, she ought to be a bit more willing to get her hands dirty. Charles's response to the detail makes us think he is naive and too keen to see in her what he wants to see.

Flaubert himself was an intriguing non-reader; or rather, his idea of reading was strange, to the point where it hardly resembled reading at all. Much as one of his characters can stare at a single line in a newspaper for a whole hour, Flaubert could lose himself in dizzy reverie, spending three days pretty much knocked out by a single scene from *King Lear*, although he seems not to have understood the plot of the play.

The author of *Madame Bovary* has always divided opinion. For some, he is the first modern novelist – and at the same time a poet among novelists. He is that rare thing, a careful visionary. (He worked slowly, taking as long over this one book as his contemporary Alexandre Dumas did over twenty-five.) For others, he is too concerned with finding precisely the right word – too fastidious, that is, about his style, about rewriting and avoiding clichés. There is a worrying strain of sadism in his writing. Moreover, his style is cold. For Proust, it brought to mind an image of a mechanical digger. Alert to the originality of this same style, Henry James thought Flaubert the 'novelist's novelist', and believed he had made the novel a more significant form, but he had misgivings about his individual works. 'There are whole sides of life', he argued, to which Flaubert's talent was never addressed, 'and which it apparently quite failed to suspect as a field of exercise'. When he met Flaubert, James found him a compelling figure, but he could still write to his own father, 'I think I easily – more than easily – see all round him intellectually.' For James, in the end, Flaubert was limited. The sceptical American, seemingly so confident of his abilities, merits a chapter of his own.

One way to talk about a nineteenth-century novel

The fiction of this period is, as I've suggested, thickly populated. So why admire one of its major characters when you can opt for someone tantalizingly obscure? You don't want to claim that your favourite is anybody as obvious as David Copperfield or Jane Eyre; instead you should choose a minor player, one of the lesser lights who memorably swells just a scene or two.

For instance, from *Bleak House* you might select old Mr Turveydrop, the 'very gentlemanly' proprietor of a dance academy, a parasite who worries that the decline of English manners has condemned his country to become 'nothing . . . but a race of weavers'. In *Middlemarch*, you could go for Mr Hawley the businessman, 'whose bad language was notorious', and who even when restraining himself possesses a 'mode of speech . . . formidable in its curtness and self-possession'. As for *Moby-Dick*, you might choose Flask the third mate, who hails from Martha's Vineyard, is 'very pugnacious concerning whales', is said to resemble a piece of short square timber, and dares not help himself to butter at the dinner table.

A few other observations about the characters who appear in nineteenth-century novels: they're always having to find time to write letters, they are apt to inflict harm on themselves, they frequently feel that their acts and words are censored, they rarely do proper jobs, they are very concerned about their parents and their heritage, and they tend to be victims of some system or philosophy that their creators wish to criticize.

13

WHO ON EARTH IS HENRY JAMES?

James was alive 1843–1916.

Major works: *The Portrait of a Lady*, *The Ambassadors*, *The Golden Bowl*.

Also wrote: numerous other novels and a large number of novellas and short stories, along with travelogues, literary criticism, memoirs and the disastrously unsuccessful play *Guy Domville*.

Trivia: more than 10,000 of the letters he wrote survive, and of these roughly a third have been published. Lamb House, his home at Rye in East Sussex, was later owned by E. F. Benson, creator of the popular 'Mapp and Lucia' novels.

A few years ago, there was a sudden glut of novels about Henry James. One of these was by David Lodge, of 'Humiliation' fame; another by Colm Tóibín, a fine Irish writer; a third by Emma Tennant, who had previously offered sequels to *Pride and Prejudice* and *Sense and Sensibility*. A fourth, by Michiel Heyns, failed to find a publisher, because, as one editor explained, 'there has just been a spate of fiction based on the life of Henry James'. Could it be, the publisher speculated, that there was 'something in the atmosphere?' As Heyns subsequently argued in a magazine article, it had always been there: the attraction of James was the 'irresistible story in the very absences of . . . [his] life' – so striking in an author 'who found his subjects in absences and suppressions'.

James, the ultimate 'writer's writer', is often referred to as The Master – the title of Tóibín's novel – and since the 1950s has become the subject of a kind of academic cult, which has positioned him as the most important of all American novelists. But of what exactly is he the master? The answer lies in what some readers will consider a fault: where Dickens and Flaubert lay a wealth of visual information before the reader, James seems comparatively fuzzy. He is more of a tentative, clue-chasing, exploratory writer, whose characters feel their way towards insights and understandings. Perhaps more than any other novelist, he suggests that big truths are seldom met head-on.

James is one those authors, like Jane Austen, who divide opinion sharply. It is hard to be indifferent to him. The reason his name comes up is that he has messianic devotees. There is a smart London book group who read nothing but James, revelling in everything that makes him difficult. And I once found myself sitting at lunch next to a bishop, who told me his idea of heaven was being a character in one of James's novels, immersed in a world of grandiose awkwardness.

But there are plenty who find James irritating: finicky, artificial, tediously interested in emotions and impressions that are always just out of reach, and overfond of the adverb 'perhaps'. The *Times Literary Supplement*'s anonymous reviewer of his novel *The Wings of the Dove* remarked that it 'will not do for short railway journeys or for drowsy hammocks', and, while praising James's achievement, conceded that 'it is not an easy book to read'. Even a scholar of James can admit that his style is sometimes 'mind-bogglingly obscure'. And if the writing is superfine, melodramatic, frustrating, the attitudes it conveys can seem over-elaborate, snobbish and painfully delicate.

Why bother with the superfine and the frustrating?

One answer is that the very qualities that make Henry James irritating also make him captivating. Among the things that link James to Jane Austen is that he writes about a narrow section of society: rich Americans, faded European aristocrats, and the landed, titled English (many of whom are actually not at all well off). Moreover, these people are chiefly interested in discussing, analysing and probing their relationships and thought processes; they are eloquent and often perceptive, but also complicated and self-destructive, and James exposes their limitations and frailties. Thus Isabel Archer in *The Portrait of a Lady* possesses a thrillingly 'immense curiosity about life', but is guilty of 'the sin of self-esteem'; Merton Densher in *The Wings of the Dove*, though 'deeply diplomatic' and 'irregularly clever', has a 'weakness . . . for life' (that is, he is better at thinking than at living); Lambert Strether in *The Ambassadors* wakens in Europe to 'the plenitude of his consciousness', and 'the cups of his impressions truly seemed to overflow', but he continues to 'live in a false world, a world that had grown simply to suit him'. James likes to write about innocents abroad, rapacious millionaires, secret affairs, people who repress their desires, and perhaps above all individuals who have to face up to a large moral responsibility.

There is, as well, a repeated contrast between the American and the European. The former is depicted as lacking complexity, cultural distinction, mystery and any very serious valuation of the past. The latter is diverse and abounds with pleasures. But Europe is also artificial and its suffocating manners can be treacherous, whereas America is a place less stifled by convention and therefore more accepting of spontaneity. In *Daisy Miller*, a tiny book that was about as close as James ever came to a bestseller, the beautiful young woman of the title is an American who is travelling in Europe. There she socializes with Winterbourne, another American, who is confused by her manners, and it is from Winterbourne's point of view that we see her. Daisy behaves in a way that he cannot fathom, which is charming but also reckless. He wonders if she is really just 'a pretty girl from New York State' or 'a designing, an audacious, an unscrupulous young person'. Daisy's manners attract the wrong kind of notice: soon her reputation is killed off by the 'bad air' of gossip, and then she succumbs to malaria (which is also, literally, bad air). *Daisy Miller* is a comedy of manners – Old World versus New – and, despite its slightness, is typical of James in the less than total reliability of its narrator and in its attention to the little nuances of relationships.

In this last department the similarity with Austen is clear, but James is more experimental and goes deeper than Austen in his treatment of the inner life. His writing reflects this, being dense, genteel, artfully constructed, sometimes deliberately opaque – exact yet ambiguous. His brother, the philosopher William James, called his style 'curly', noting that 'you can't skip a word'. Take, for instance, the opening of *The Portrait of a Lady*: 'Under certain circumstances there are few hours in life more agreeable than the hour dedicated to the ceremony known as afternoon tea.' There follows a description of one particular tea:

> The implements of the little feast had been disposed upon the lawn of an old English country house, in what I should call the perfect middle of a splendid summer afternoon. Part of the afternoon had waned, but much of it was left, and what was left was of the finest and rarest quality. Real dusk would not arrive for many hours; but the flood of summer light had begun to ebb, the air had grown mellow, the shadows were long upon the smooth, dense turf.

And then:

> The shadows on the perfect lawn were straight and angular; they were the shadows of an old man sitting in a deep wicker chair near the low table on which the tea had been served, and of two younger men strolling to and fro, in desultory talk, in front of him. The old man had his cup in his hand; it was an unusually large cup, of a different pattern from the rest of the set and painted in brilliant colours. He disposed of its contents with much circumspection, holding it for a long time close to his chin, with his face turned to the house.

The opening of *The Portrait* reads like stage directions for a play. It also seems prissy. But the language James uses evokes the pompous nature of the occasion and its rituals. The repetitions of 'disposed' and 'perfect' are calculated. James is, I think, delicately satirizing the mechanical excellence of a fine tea. A world twice touched (in different places) with the adjective 'perfect' is not likely to be perfect at all. The disposals – of the 'implements of the little feast' and of the contents of the old man's unusually large cup – are anything but casual.

Some other classic openings

1. 'Many years later, as he faced the firing squad, Colonel Aureliano Buendia was to remember that distant afternoon when his father took him to discover ice' (Gabriel García Márquez, *One Hundred Years of Solitude*)

2. 'It was a queer, sultry summer, the summer they electrocuted the Rosenbergs, and I didn't know what I was doing in New York' (Sylvia Plath, *The Bell Jar*)

3. 'I was born in the year 1632, in the city of York, of a good family, though not of that county, my father being a foreigner of Bremen, who settled first at Hull' (Daniel Defoe, *Robinson Crusoe*)

4. 'It was a bright cold day in April, and the clocks were striking thirteen' (George Orwell, *1984*)

5. 'Whether I shall turn out to be the hero of my life, or whether that station will be held by anybody else, these pages must show' (Dickens, *David Copperfield*)

6. 'In my younger and more vulnerable years my father gave me some advice that I've been turning over in my mind ever since' (F. Scott Fitzgerald, *The Great Gatsby*)

7. 'It was a wrong number that started it, the telephone ringing three times in the dead of night, and the voice on the other end asking for someone he was not' (Paul Auster, *City of Glass*)

The Portrait of a Lady is another of the books I had to read at school, and I remember one of my classmates groaning, 'You can tell the bugger never had a shag' – perhaps not the most Jamesian choice of words, but shrewd in its way, as James was celibate. It was the same classmate who drew my attention to a line in Chapter 49: 'Madame Merle slowly got up, stroking her muff.' Good stuff with which to enliven a slow double lesson.

H. G. Wells likened James's style to the spectacle of a 'magnificent but painful hippopotamus resolved at any cost, even at the cost of its dignity, upon picking up a pea which has got into a corner of its den'. Its phrasing is effortful. In James's notoriously difficult late novels, he keeps interrupting himself and uses very knotty syntax. Here, for example, is a passage in *The Golden Bowl*, in which Amerigo, a penniless Italian prince, is being described, from the point of view of Fanny Assingham, who is a typical Jamesian observer of other people's existences:

> His look . . . suggested an image – that of some very noble personage who, expected, acclaimed by the crowd in the street and with old precious stuffs falling over the sill for his support, had gaily and gallantly come to show himself: always moreover less in his own interest than in that of spectators and subjects whose need to admire, even to gape, was periodically to be considered. The young man's expression became after this fashion something vivid and concrete – a beautiful personal presence, that of a prince in very truth, a ruler, warrior, patron, lighting up brave architecture and diffusing the sense of a function. It had been happily said of his face that the figure thus appearing in the great frame was the ghost of some proudest ancestor.

This is all pretty drawn out, and it is deliberately so. The language of morality is being stretched. At the point where the description comes, the reader is aware that Amerigo is going to be married to an American heiress, Maggie Verver. In due course they do marry, and, at Maggie's urging, her millionaire father marries Amerigo's former lover, the accomplished Charlotte Stant. The thinking here is that, with Maggie married, Mr Verver will be lonely; he needs a companion of his own. In practice, though, he and Maggie grow closer after the two marriages, and Amerigo and Charlotte are also together more, joined by (among other things) their relish of life's ironies. What follows hardly needs describing, except to say that in the end Maggie diplomatically achieves the revival of both marriages. Of more immediate concern is the way this description of Amerigo plays a part in showing the layers of his character. What is there here that suggests Amerigo will be a deceiver? Notice the attention to his exterior, to his self-display out of concern for his admirers, to his transmitting 'the sense of a function'. Which details perhaps suggest a hint of something unsavoury in Mrs Assingham's image of him?

The characters in James's novels are not obviously interesting. Many are stale, refined, unemphatic; austere, modest or weak-willed. But they are interesting nevertheless, because James himself is so interested in them. He called his characters 'my agitated friends'. Their motives are analysed, and so are the revisions of opinion and judgement that result from experience. There is a sense, with all James's characters, that they are yet to be fully formed. His skill lies in showing us the ordeals of undeveloped consciousness.

In his essay 'The Art of Fiction', James argued against what he saw as a false distinction between the 'novel of incident' and the 'novel of character'. Instead of crediting this divide, we should understand that 'character is action'. This idea can in fact be traced back as far as Aristotle, and it is manifest across all times and genres – certainly not just in James's 'novels of intelligence', but also in the very earliest fictional works.

14

TWO 'UNREADABLES': *DON QUIXOTE* AND *THE TALE OF GENJI*

Miguel de Cervantes, author of *Don Quixote*, lived from 1547 to 1616. His other works include a number of so-called 'exemplary' stories – superficially didactic, but really satirical – and several plays. His name is pronounced *therr-van-tez*. His most famous book is *don kee-ho-tay*.

Murasaki Shikibu is the pen name of the author of *The Tale of Genji*. She is reckoned to have been born around 973 in Kyoto. The date of her death is unclear, but 1014 is usually suggested.

Trivia: 'Murasaki' means 'purple wisteria blossom'. Cervantes was a purchasing agent responsible for securing provisions such as grain and oil for the Spanish Armada.

Imagine, if you will, a long, episodic novel about a retired gent in his fifties, who is overcome by a passion for books full of derring-do. His brain dries up, he loses his wits, and he decides to set out on an adventure of the kind described in his favourite literature. He puts on an old suit of armour, changes his name, saddles up his horse (also freshly named for the occasion), fastens his desire on a local farm girl, and recruits a feckless neighbour to be his sidekick, enticing him with the promise that he will become governor of an 'island' (the word is unknown to the sidekick). Then off they go, after something of a false start, and the delusions continue apace. The middle-aged knight attacks some windmills, thinking they are giants, and is knocked to the ground by one of their sails; clearly the fates intervened to deny him the satisfaction of victory. Staying at an inn, he convinces himself it is an enchanted castle. He thinks the clouds of dust raised by two flocks of sheep are two armies – one Christian, one Muslim – on the brink of battle. He attacks a man he thinks is a knight sporting a famous golden helmet; in fact it is an itinerant barber wearing his shaving basin on his head. When his ear is damaged in a quarrel over the honour of a lady, he insists that as a knight-errant he should not complain of a wound received in battle, but he notices (twice) that the injury hurts more than he can bear; it is later cured by a goatherd, with an ointment containing spittle, salt and rosemary.

The novel of which I have just provided a crude and incomplete snapshot is Miguel de Cervantes' *Don Quixote*. There are several reasons why this book, originally *El Ingenioso Hidalgo Don Quixote de la Mancha*, is a cultural touchstone. It is commonly regarded as the first modern novel. By writing about ordinary people, Cervantes suggested something of the heroism of everyday life. His novel is cited as a strong influence on Dickens, Flaubert and Dostoevsky, among many. It is also, in effect, an anthology of all the styles of literature that were to be found in Spain at a time when that country was one of the dominant world powers. For a long period it helped forge international perceptions of Spain and the Spanish. Visitors to Spain will be familiar with the wealth of merchandise related to the novel: statuettes, playing cards, corkscrews, calendars, dolls, glassware, and plenty besides. The word 'quixotic' has entered fairly common usage; it denotes a person who is quick to act, a touch naive, impractical, unrealistic. It is worth bearing in mind as well that the novel's two volumes were published in the first two decades of the seventeenth century – the age of Shakespeare, and indeed of Galileo.

The style of *Don Quixote* seems less archaic than that of most literature of its time. Although it is difficult, it can feel surprisingly forward-looking, most of all in its concern with the responsibilities that have to be assumed by the individual. In the nineteenth century Cervantes' novel was hijacked by the German Romantics, who chose to think of it not as a comedy, but as bittersweet, ironic and avant-garde. Plenty of readers today are struck by what can seem its troublingly prescient picture of the random violence, bumbling manners and energetic vulgarity of the modern world.

Nonetheless, there are obstacles to a relaxed appreciation of Cervantes' novel. Martin Amis comments, 'While clearly an impregnable masterpiece, *Don Quixote* suffers from one fairly serious flaw – that of outright unreadability.' Conceding that the book abounds with moments of charm and comedy, Amis nonetheless deems it 'for long stretches . . . inhumanly dull'. This is partly because Cervantes seems to have thought that if a thing was worth saying it was worth saying repeatedly. Nothing happens – several times.

Amis is not alone in finding *Don Quixote* unreadable. It frequently figures in lists of classic works that readers have failed to grapple into submission. *Ulysses* and *À la recherche* are also regulars. But a little digging, among my friends and beyond, disclosed some other, less obvious 'unreadables': *Wuthering Heights*, *American Psycho*, *Gulliver's Travels*, anything by Hemingway, *The Lord of the Rings*, anything by the sex-fixated novelist Henry Miller, most of Thomas Mann, and every single self-help book from St Augustine to Rhonda Byrne's *The Secret*.

Cervantes apparently considered brevity a virtue, but his novel hardly bears this out. The chapter titles give the flavour: 'Which recounts the amusing manner in which Don Quixote was dubbed a knight', 'In which note is made of the braying adventure and the diverting adventure of the puppet master, along with the memorable divinations of the soothsaying monkey', 'Regarding the most incomparable and singular adventure ever concluded . . .', 'Regarding certain things . . . and others that are really quite remarkable'. All those praise-laden adjectives – which feel like the work of an estate agent – call up a suspicion, as each chapter begins, that what we are about to read is not so very diverting and memorable. The chapter titles may be touched with irony, but *Don Quixote* resembles one of those interior-design projects that start out with a clear vision and end up overstuffed with décor.

At times, even the author sounds as though he is yawning. Don Quixote is 'wonderfully regaled', 'dumbfounded' (repeatedly), 'extremely melancholy on the one hand and very happy

on the other', and so on. One night, staying at the inn he
believes is a castle, he hallucinates and slashes the wineskins that
hang at the head of his bed, thinking all the while that he is
locked in combat with a giant. He is discovered 'in the strangest
outfit in the world', which turns out to involve nothing
stranger than a greasy red nightcap. A small embarrassment
takes pages to be explained, and the apologies and consolations
that follow require several pages more.

Inconveniently, too, Don Quixote is polite; when he meets
someone boring, he allows the bore to waffle on without interruption. The novel contains a great deal of dialogue. Don
Quixote sees the world very differently from his sidekick
Sancho Panza – and from everyone else, for that matter – and
the differences are played out in a sustained conversation that is
frequently affectionate and humorous, but is also tetchy,
dejected and pathetically self-justifying. Sancho tends to do a
lot of listening, while his master does the speaking. (The relationship has been likened to those between Batman and Robin,
Laurel and Hardy, and Abbott and Costello.) The longer the
novel goes on, the more space is given to talk. And what talk it
is. Here is Don Quixote, about two-thirds of the way through:
'Now I say . . . that the man who reads a good deal and travels
a good deal, sees a good deal and knows a good deal.' Surely
not! But this is the kind of thing he keeps saying.

Tellingly, the famous bits of *Don Quixote* are near the start.
The novel begins wonderfully (here in Edith Grossman's
admirable translation):

Somewhere in La Mancha, in a place whose name I do not care
to remember, a gentleman lived not long ago, one of those who

has a lance and ancient shield on a shelf and a skinny nag and a greyhound for racing. An occasional stew, beef more often than lamb, hash most nights, eggs and abstinence on Saturdays, lentils on Fridays, sometimes squab as a treat on Sundays – these consumed three-fourths of his income.

Those details sing! The greyhound, ready to be raced, and the notes on Don Quixote's diet. Initially, too, the spectacle of his misadventures is amusing, as his romantic ideals collide with day-to-day reality. But when, after several hundred pages, the misadventures seem barely to have changed – when Don Quixote still seems to know what he is doing, and we still don't – even an indulgent reader may want to put the book to one side. Absurd events are explained carefully and rationally, only for the idea that there is such a thing as objective truth to be undermined. Experiencing this again and again is rather too much like being told repeatedly why we ought to have laughed at something we've failed to find funny. The novel has two parts, and the second part – written after a man calling himself Alonso de Avellaneda had brought out a bogus sequel – is less digressive than the first, but the joke has by then worn thin.

This distaste of mine is, of course, all very heretical. There are people who would smite me rather more than just quixotically for my insolence. But that is the sort of thing you ought to want to happen. It is the sort of thing about which Cervantes could have written a long, sloppy, fitfully amusing book.

Cervantes is a founding figure, a pioneer of the novel, and *Don Quixote* raises many of the concerns that today engage lovers of fiction. For instance, while some readers expect the principal characters in novels to be likeable, there is a powerful opposing view that the most interesting characters are – as in *Don Quixote* – morally ambiguous. People who read novels are frequently nagged by other suspicions: that all novels are historical novels, have their roots in autobiography, are experimental, betray particular political values, are mysteries, manifest a self-consciousness about their status as fiction, are collaborations, have unsatisfactory endings, and are erotic. Any of these statements, taken on its own, is a suitable point of departure for a sustaining argument. It is worth adding, I think, that when novels became popular in the early eighteenth century, in no small part influenced by Cervantes' achievement, they were seen as an upstart form – subversive because democratic, anarchic, trashy, impure and not in verse.

But *Don Quixote*, like many classics, intimidates with its sheer bulk. Loafing in a good bookshop, I check the number of pages in several editions: 1,056; 992; 1,048; 1,120. I don't think it's churlish to say that that is a lot of text to have to get through. Pick up a copy of *Middlemarch* or *Moby-Dick*: it feels hard to handle, awkward. If the copy you are holding is a paperback, you know you will have at some point to break its spine. You do it, and the glue seems to sneer at you from between its pages. You can't hold it open with a single hand, and when you have held it for a while your arm begins to ache.

There are volumes of which this is even more dismayingly true. Confronted with an unabridged edition of Samuel Richardson's *Clarissa*, a reader might fancy she will need to get planning permission in order to read it outdoors. (It amounts to more than a million words and was originally published in eight separate volumes.) As a teenager, I was caught with a copy by an older and apparently wiser soul, who groaned, 'What are you reading that for?' He assessed my disappointment before going on: 'Don't bother. It'll just slow you down.' There is, of course, something to be said for slowing down, as suggested by Proust.

Most books cost more to read than to buy, and this is especially true of lengthy classics available in cheap editions. I can acquire *Moby-Dick* for a few pounds, and in doing so can receive its creator's gift of pleasure, but it will take me many hours to read it. How much is my time worth? Let us say I think it is worth no more than the basic minimum wage, and let us suppose that I am a fast reader: the cost of reading it is still, I could argue, £50. The rewards may well justify the expense, but this explains, I think, why people who do read almost invariably own a great many books that they have nevertheless not got around to reading.

One book that looked down at me forbiddingly for a long time before I plucked up the resolve to peek inside its covers was *The Tale of Genji*, a novel which is both an early masterpiece of imaginative writing – long before *Don Quixote* – and a valuable testament to the life, a millennium ago, of the Japanese court. It is usually credited to a woman who was a member of the aristocratic Fujiwara family, powerful in tenth-century Japan. Her nickname is Murasaki Shikibu. *The Tale of Genji* has more in common with English novels of the nineteenth century than it does with the works that were being produced in Europe at the time when it was written – works such as *Beowulf* and *The Song of Roland*, that is, which are concerned with knights' heroic valour. Lady Murasaki's novel is a historical curio. Its language is far removed from modern Japanese, but some of its psychological insights are easily grasped and enjoyed.

The *Genji* is really two tales. The first, melancholy yet beautiful, occupies forty of the book's fifty-four chapters, and tells of the life and loves of Hikaru Genji, a gifted and handsome embodiment of 'shining' masculine virtue. Genji is the son of the Emperor by one of his concubines. The Emperor loves Genji, and would be thrilled to make him his heir, but he knows this would never wash with the imperial court, and so, instead, Genji is given a surname (Minamoto) and removed from the imperial household so that he can enjoy a career in government. Genji climbs the ladder of office. His skills impress, and above all he is skilled in the art of love. He has a tendency to tangle himself in difficult affairs, and there are times when he prowls like a hunter, but his sensitivity is acute, and his fine sensibility means he is often disappointed by life – fond, but sad. Then, after forty chapters in this vein, Chapter 41 is 'blank': Genji dies, and the next section begins 'His light was gone, and none among his many descendants could compare to what he had been.' The second, shorter part of the novel follows – a view of the generation who serve at court after Genji's death. This section is touched by doubt about the future of the sophisticated courtier class. Perishability is a motif of Japanese art and culture – think of the pleasure taken in the cherry blossom that dies within a few days of flowering – and the exquisiteness of the impermanent is tangible in Murasaki's novel.

One of its most celebrated moments involves the teenage Genji, one wet evening, listening in on a triangular conversation about women. The three participants are courtiers (male, naturally, and all young); the talk they share resembles a million locker-room exchanges since, though it is more decorous as well as more ruminative. The three men converse about feminine wiles, the merits of an immature and docile wife you can mould to suit your needs, the importance of finding a dependable companion, the corrosive power of jealousy, the dangers of being with a forward or easy woman, a woman's capacity for appearing serene when actually she is hurt, and the advantages for a woman in pretending to be less intelligent than she is. It all rings true.

However, the *Genji* is a long novel; the unabridged and annotated translation that I have – the work of Royall Tyler – runs to well over 1,000 pages. At times it is peculiarly intimate, and many who sample it find themselves quickly absorbed by its picture of polite rivalries, its subtle eroticism and its exposure of the tension between religious aspirations and day-to-day responsibilities. In Tyler's scrupulous version, the reputedly intricate drama of the original often comes across well. But there is a good deal in the novel that seems cold.

There are reasons for this, to do with its aristocratic milieu. Take, for instance, these moments from a chapter in which Genji tries to rekindle his relationship with Fujitsubo, one of his father's consorts, who some years previously bore him a son: 'A proud complacency had made him somewhat indifferent to her,' 'As he laid his whole complaint before her, his eyes on a sky perhaps lovelier still now that the moon had set, all the bitterness pent up in his heart melted away,' 'An icy wind was blowing, and the pine crickets' faltering song so truly caught the mood of the moment that not even someone free of care could have heard it without a pang.' The language here is evasive and discreet in a manner suited not only to the social class of those involved, but also to the subject matter. Repressed emotion and the awkwardness of diplomacy are rendered with frigid elegance. Prose was, in the age of Murasaki, something fairly new in Japanese, and it was typically written by women. Moreover, it was associated with privacy. Murasaki's prose is hemmed in by the honour code of her upper-class culture. By contrast, the 795 poems interspersed through the novel's pages, while often conventional, are expressions of the inner life, personal and individual.

Nonetheless, the trouble with a novel in which emotional expression seems stymied, and which is full of wrong turns and hesitations, is that it risks alienating the reader. The *Genji* may be a story of romantic intrigue, but it is intrigue of the most sedate kind. It embodies some of the more puzzling features of Japanese art: *sabi*, the mixture of beauty and desolation that one tastes in the ripeness of deep loneliness, and *yugen*, a dark ethereal grace which cannot be expressed directly and lies, never perfectly known, far beneath the surface of things.

The Tale of Genji has been interpreted as a work of Buddhist mysticism, a historical record of a tiny lost world, a feminist criticism of men's sexual conduct, and even a satirical picture of the decadence of the aristocracy. It has also been seen as promoting the idea of a higher existence we can aspire to – and which it is worth our aspiring to. In the end, though, the most remarkable thing about this 'tale' is that it was produced at a time when the king of England was Cnut and the Scottish king was Macbeth. As Virginia Woolf quirkily put it, 'While the Aelfrics and the Aelfreds croaked and coughed in England, this court lady . . . was sitting down in a silk dress . . . with flowers in her garden and nightingales in the trees.'

15

THE OTHER OLD TALES: AESOP, CHAUCER AND THE ARABIAN NIGHTS

'Mummy, what's the difference between a story and a tale?'

'Um . . . A story tells you about something that happened: a tale isn't really that different, but it's got magic in it, too.'

I was browsing in a bookshop – a self-consciously quaint one, near where I live – when I heard this exchange between a mother and her son, who was about six years old. I am not sure the distinction would be all that widely accepted (it does just about work for the *Genji*), but to me at the time it seemed interesting. The magical terrain of tales is a representation of the Unconscious.

The name to drop at this point is Bruno Bettelheim, whose classic study *The Uses of Enchantment* presents fairy tales as accounts of life's essential problems – and as solutions to those problems, capable of fostering personal development. Thus the tale of Little Red Riding Hood, the most popular version of which is recorded by Jacob and Wilhelm Grimm, dramatizes the tension between doing what one ought to do – staying on the path – and doing what one would like to do – straying off into the forest to pick flowers. Furthermore, Little Red Riding Hood's ambivalent relationship with the wolf – in Gustave Doré's famous illustration, they are seen in bed together, and she seems both horrified and fascinated by the wolf – suggests something of a pubescent girl's typical ambivalence about sex, a cause of both anxiety and curiosity. There is plenty more to be said about the tale of Little Red Riding Hood, but Bettelheim's main point is this: tales highlight the truth that life is intrinsically difficult, and they also show that difficulties can be overcome.

Part of the attraction of tales is, I think, that they contain ordinary protagonists, whose quests often reflect ours: the desire to belong, to find something that has been lost, to confront fears. Yet their appeal depends also on their archaic elements: the beating of a unicorn's hooves, salty sea voyages, ivy-wrapped towers, or talking dogs, hovering carpets and cloaks that make the wearer invisible. A tale tends to project us into another time, and can do so quite explicitly – 'Once upon a time, a very long time ago, in the reign of King Log'; that sort of thing. It lifts us out of our familiar space. We move into a realm of fantasy, but it is one which retains qualities that we recognize. In C. S. Lewis's Narnia there are centaurs, wood spirits and marsh-wiggles with leathery skin, but also four quite ordinary children for whom the illusion of childhood as a sort of golden age burns bright. Similarly, in Alice's Wonderland – even though eating a mushroom can make a person grow, pebbles turn into cakes, and croquet is played with flamingos as mallets and hedgehogs as balls – there are enmities and jealousies with which every reader can identify. These constructions are both parallel worlds and eminently real ones; the extraordinary events and weird creatures seem perfectly valid facets of experience.

There is a noticeable difference between tales and fables. In this second category the most famous examples are *Aesop's Fables*, an assortment of short tales geared towards moral education, credited to a Greek slave who lived during the sixth century BC. Some of these tales have become proverbial: the boy who cried 'wolf', the hare and the tortoise, the goose that laid the golden eggs, the wolf in sheep's clothing. So, for instance, we have the little fable of the fox and the leopard. The two of them decided to conduct a beauty contest. The leopard was boastful, pointing out how wonderfully varied his coat was. The fox retorted, 'I am so much more beautiful than you are, for I have variety not just in my body, but also in soul.' Or we have the fable of the goat and the vine, where, as the vine buds deliciously, the goat chews its fresh shoots. The vine says, 'Why are you doing damage to me like this? Don't imagine I'll provide any less wine when the time comes for you to be sacrificed!' *Aesop's Fables* are a little heavy-handed in conveying their moral message. Nothing is held back. By contrast, fairy tales leave the decision-making to their audience. Part of this, as Bettelheim says, is whether we wish to make any decision at all. By being more open-ended, tales endow their audience with freedom. This is of particular value when that audience consists of children, who learn from tales about the powers they have as well as about those that they will have in the future.

To succeed as entertainment, tales must be enchanting, and to succeed in being educative, they must contain conflict. This is conspicuous in *The Thousand and One Nights* (or the *Arabian Nights*, as it is often known), in which moral messages are couched in a charming style, with tensions and travails built into smartly contrived plots that usually urge reasonableness, politeness and an awareness of life's limits. It is easy to think of the *Arabian Nights* as a clutter of kitsch fragments, stuffed with genies, baskets of snakes and people in floaty trousers. Yes, there are devious sorcerers and skulking thieves, dark doorways, books impregnated with poison, fish that can talk and clouds of sweet-smelling incense, but there are also accounts of life and death that get to the very heart of what makes storytelling so powerful. This is a book of wonders, but there is more to it than just the fruity scent of pleasure.

It used to be claimed in parts of the Middle East that if you read the whole of the *Arabian Nights* you would die. As much a part of Western literature as of Eastern, it was popularized in Europe by Antoine Galland, a French archaeologist whose translation of the tales filled a dozen volumes. Galland's exceptionally large collection is now known in abridged form. The popular version by Husain Haddawy covers about a quarter of the tales. The most famous of these is probably the larger story that frames the rest. King Shahriyar (the name is Persian) finds out that his wife has been unfaithful to him with a servant who works in his kitchens. He has her put to death. Henceforth, he decides to sleep only with virgins; each will spend a single night with him, and will then be executed in the morning. Scheherazade, the daughter of the Persian vizier, suggests herself as one of Shahriyar's one-night tricks, much to the horror of her father. Once installed in the king's chamber, she contrives to break the pattern. She does this by arranging to tell him a story after they have had sex, and by ensuring that she does not finish it that night. The King, curious to know more, keeps her alive. The next night the story goes on, but is not completed, and Scheherazade begins a new one. So it continues for nearly three years. And by the time she finally leaves off her story-telling, she has given birth to several children by Shahriyar, leading him to renounce his murderous intentions.

In reality, this collection brings together tales that have their origins in Egypt, Persia, Syria and India. The names of their authors are not known. The collection contains fairy tales, along with cautionary fables, debates, poetry, piety and some bits bordering on porn. A number of the stories have, like that of Scheherazade, become very well known. (In common with Don Quixote, Scheherazade has been the inspiration for a famous ballet.) Many people are familiar with the rags-to-riches story of Aladdin and the lamp, especially in its simplified pantomime form. Ditto Ali Baba and the Forty Thieves. Sindbad the Sailor is another familiar name, though the details of his seven voyages tend to be recalled only very dimly. Like Aladdin, Sindbad has many times been re-imagined, and in popular versions of his story he is often a piratical adventurer rather than a poor porter working in Baghdad. In the original the salient feature of Sindbad's voyages is their hazardous nature, reflecting the boundlessness of his desire to see the world. Sindbad embodies the idea that there is no gain in life without some pain – and the verso of this, the idea that all life's pains result in gains. Generally, the tales that make up the *Arabian Nights* promote a simple moral: virtue will be rewarded, and misdeeds will be punished.

It is possible that, in oral form, the stories from this Arabian collection found their way to the England of Geoffrey Chaucer. Certainly, Chaucer in *The Canterbury Tales* employs some of the techniques found in the *Arabian Nights*, and he includes a few details that seem to have their origins in Arab sources – such as a flying horse made of brass and a female falcon who talks of being deserted by her mate. But Chaucer's tales are segments of a unified whole, and, while each of them offers its own vision and can be seen as a literary experiment, Chaucer's imprint on all of them is clear. He drew on numerous foreign sources, but added to them an original drama and humour, creating characters of vibrant complexity.

Why do people study Geoffrey Chaucer?

The Canterbury Tales is an unfinished collection of stories supposedly told by a group of thirty pilgrims travelling from London to Canterbury. These pilgrims represent the breadth of medieval society. The cast contains, among others, a crusader knight, a dainty prioress, a lawyer, a rascally old sea-dog, a physician, a prosperous merchant, a cook with a nasty sore on his shin, a devout parson, a suspiciously well-dressed monk, a rambunctious miller, and a fraudulent seller of papal indulgences. Chaucer impersonates these pilgrims' different voices, and every tale suits its teller. *The Canterbury Tales* contains a good deal about sex, money, love and religion. A broad portrait of fourteenth-century England, it sheds light on the mercantile, military and spiritual aspects of society, as well as on the emergence of a new middle class. And many of the questions Chaucer raises – about the different roles of men and women, or about the relationship between dreams, fears and creativity – still feel pertinent more than 600 years after they were asked.

Chaucer's language, Middle English, looks tricky. Try this, for instance: 'Our manciple, I hope he wil be deed, / Swa

werkes ay the wanges in his heed.' Some of the words are familiar, but anyone could be forgiven for being baffled by 'swa' and
'wanges', as well as for wondering if 'I hope he wil be deed'
means quite what it sounds as though it should. His poetry
repays a bit of courage. The experience of reading it aloud can
be entertaining, but it's not as if anyone is going to sit you down
and ask you to read aloud from *The Canterbury Tales*. Rather,
the main concern is to understand what someone means in
describing a character or a situation as Chaucerian. While
Chaucer is capable of sounding self-consciously literary – his

---

Three Chaucerian bits of naughtiness

1. In *The Miller's Tale*, a foppish clerk calls one night on the
   young woman with whom he's smitten. He knocks on
   her window, expecting to receive a kiss, and is stunned
   instead to find himself kissing 'hir naked ers'.

2. In *The Reeve's Tale*, told in retaliation for the story told by
   the Miller, two Cambridge students revenge themselves
   on a greedy miller who has been ripping off their college.
   In the night they find their way into the beds of his wife
   and daughter. One of them, John, addresses the wife in
   terms that hardly need translation: 'He priketh harde and
   depe, as he were mad.'

3. In *The Merchant's Tale*, May, the fragrant wife of a crabbed
   old man called Januarie, cheats on him by having sex in a
   pear tree with Damyan, one of the squires in his service.
   Damyan is memorably pictured seizing the, er, moment:
   'Gan pullen up the smok, and in he throng.'

---

long poem *Troilus and Criseyde* is courtly and often laden with polysyllables – his name usually conjures the mood of his bawdier tales: earthy, crafty and humorous, with a sort of easy flair, and reminiscent of a whole very English type of comedy, full of mishaps, sweet revenges and innuendoes. When anyone speaks of a 'Chaucerian' character, the image is of a person real, corruptible and full of energy and talk. More often, the word is intended to call to mind a mood: an air of fun, knowing yet fresh; a delight in life that can appear naive but is nothing of the sort; and a lightly worn seriousness.

It's rare to encounter someone who first came to Chaucer outside the classroom or the lecture theatre. When he is fun, he is very good fun, but he is pigeonholed as someone whose works need to be taught. If you took *The Canterbury Tales* to the beach, people would think you had gone bananas. The same goes for *The Faerie Queene* or *Paradise Lost*. I know someone who in a job interview was asked which figure from the past she would most like to have met. Her reply – 'Chaucer' – was a curveball. You're supposed to say Winston Churchill or Isaac Newton or Muhammad or Jesus, aren't you? (Or Florence Nightingale. Or Marco Polo.) The decision to say Chaucer's name was a good one; my friend got the job. But you can be sure that the interviewer smiled at the idea: Chaucer seems about as real as Winnie the Pooh.

Because Chaucer is a 'taught' author, he's often wrapped up in jargon, so this seems an appropriate place to say something about scholarly lingo. You can usually tell someone who has 'studied literature' because he or she – but let's for brevity's sake say *he* – avoids straightforward judgements such as 'I really liked the first 200 pages of *David Copperfield*' (how gauche!),

HOW TO REALLY TALK ABOUT BOOKS YOU HAVEN'T READ

preferring instead to talk about the novel's 'incorporation of agonistic socio-cultural restraints'. In fact, words like 'book' and 'novel' are out; 'text', 'discourse' and 'literary production' are the order of the day. Texts get 'interrogated'. Meanings are 'sedimentary'. Basic ideas and positions are 'problematized'. Different theories of how they should be interrogated are bundled up as 'hermeneutics'. The professorial reader has been trained to look for things that most people cannot see, like 'intertextuality' – the way literature grows out of other literature or is a mosaic of allusions. Jargon is academics' way of showing that their study of literature is scientific and has the rigour of philosophy.

I'm being a hypocrite, because I've used these words myself – but not all at the same time. In any case, not everyone who talks like this is totally insufferable, and in some circumstances it may help you too to drop in a buzzword of this kind. Yet by and large jargon-lovers, while possibly less intelligent than they imagine or wish you to think, do know what they are on about, and you may be better off discussing football, food or shoes, subjects on which they will also talk mystifyingly but much less impressively. Their weird hubris is usefully summed up in a joke I've heard about a college lecturer who, asked whether he has read a certain new book, exclaims, 'Read it? I haven't even lectured on it yet!' Weak though it is, this is a joke every examinee should bear in mind: don't be too reverent of the examination process, or of what you are being examined on, because the people examining you are irreverent about the whole business. But when I shared this joke with a friend recently, he darted off in a different direction: 'That's no literary critic. Your guy sounds like a philosopher.'

How to talk about writing

Writing is a craft. It's a process. It's a drug. It's a code. It's a journey. It's often a feat of typing as much as of invention. (These are all things I have read or heard.) It's like carpentry, painting, gem-setting or dance. It is a conversation. It's a love letter to the rest of the world. It is an act of discovery. It is a negotiation between author and reader. It is a way of storing information. It is at once a discipline and a form of freedom. All writing is creative. All writing is personal. All writing is rewriting.

If you detect a certain weariness here, you are right to do so. We write to empty our minds. We write to reveal ourselves and yet also to mask ourselves. We write because in doing so we get a better hold on life. But from all such statements there comes a whiff of cheese. The first rule, actually, is this: read over whatever you write, and when you come across something you're particularly impressed with, delete it.

16

HOW DO YOU GET A PHILOSOPHER OFF YOUR DOORSTEP?

Not long ago, I found myself on a stag weekend being harangued by a fellow guest – hardly known to me – who wanted to have a 'serious' conversation. 'Which philosopher has influenced you the most?' he asked. I concentrated my attentions on my soggy pizza. 'Come on, I mean it. Who's *really* influenced you?' I may at this point have suppressed a yawn. 'Because for me it has to be Nietzsche. He's The Man – don't you think?'

My reluctance to be drawn on the issue clearly marked me out as a philistine, and an unfriendly one at that. One reason for not thinking that Nietzsche is The Man is that his philosophy, admittedly after some distortions, appealed so strongly to Nazis, Jew-haters and other opponents of egalitarianism. Furthermore, he so obviously thought he *was* The Man ('I have a terrible fear that I shall one day be pronounced *holy*,' 'To take a book of mine into his hands is one of the rarest distinctions that anyone can confer upon himself.'). But, actually, what this exchange put me in mind of was a story a friend once told, about seeing, in one of the grimier parts of South London, a blacked-out car with 'I'm The Man' emblazoned across its side in bright yellow. My friend approached the car to see who exactly The Man might be. The driver's window inched down. It certainly wasn't Nietzsche, because the driver was too curt even for that most quotably succinct of philosophers: 'What the FUCK OFF.' In any case, Nietzsche (the first syllable is pronounced like *knee*, and the second sounds like *tshuh*, an expression of disgruntlement) died in 1900 – of pneumonia, syphilis or brain cancer, according to whose propaganda you believe.

When I was a teenager, a burdensomely earnest conversation was known as 'a deep' – as in 'Ben and Dave are having a deep'. Having a deep consisted of discussing one's emotions or, in a moment of eye-watering pretentiousness, debating a question raised by a philosopher – or at least by one of the philosophical *bons mots* presented in the *Oxford Dictionary of Quotations*. Sometimes a deep wasn't very deep at all ('How much money would it take for you to have sex with a stranger on a plane?'), but it could be more profound: are judgements about art nothing more than a matter of taste, are the claims we make about ethics really any more than emotional positions, is there any circumstance under which it is acceptable to torture someone? The answer to the last of these is obviously 'Yes, if they make you talk about Nietzsche while your Quattro Formaggi is getting cold.'

Teenage philosophers adore Nietzsche. The German's aphorisms make him wonderfully quotable: 'No price is too high to pay for the privilege of owning yourself,' 'Distrust all in whom the impulse to punish is powerful,' 'Morality is herd instinct in the individual,' or just 'God is dead.' This is all jolly useful when you're arguing with your parents about why you should be allowed to get your tongue pierced, but Nietzsche has become an icon of adolescent disgruntlement, a name to drop unreflectingly along with Che Guevara and, like, you know, Andy Warhol.

Adulthood poses different challenges. Perhaps I am a lightweight, but I have very rarely found myself really needing to be able to talk about philosophers. Life may be enriched – made interestingly complicated – by reading Thomas Aquinas or the Danish philosopher Søren Kierkegaard, but they don't make many appearances in casual chat, and in fact they seldom come up even in serious conversation. Nevertheless, it's worth having some sort of strategy for the occasions when philosophical debate does rear its head.

One-sentence simplifications of the arguments of particular philosophers are laughably inadequate. But let's quickly have a few, anyway. Aristotle, who spent two decades as Plato's student, suggested that all humans desire *eudaimonia* – that is, to flourish, to be happy, to be in a state of perpetual and blissful activity, tantamount to success. René Descartes famously wrote 'Cogito ergo sum', which is usually translated as 'I think therefore I am,' but could be more helpfully translated as 'I am thinking, therefore I am,' since Descartes argues that one can be sure one exists only when one is actually thinking. John Locke put forward the idea that our knowledge is made up of information gathered by our five senses; in other words, everything comes from experience, and we are born without any already defined values and principles. David Hume challenged the notion that humans are particularly rational; all ideas are copies of impressions, and where many imagine there to be certainties there are only probabilities. Immanuel Kant, my buddy who did not in fact have very much to do with the platypus, advanced the argument – alarming to his contemporaries – that when we perceive the world around us our perceptions are tinted by attributes of our individual minds. There would have been no Kantian philosophy without Hume, and probably no Hume without Locke, and no Locke without Descartes. Georg Hegel, whose work picked up where Kant left off (with some explicit criticism of Kant), proposed a 'dialectical' method of scholarly writing – which also served as a model of the workings of the world – in which a norm (the status quo, or some accepted idea) is broken down by an opposing force (such as a new way of thinking), and this confrontation between 'thesis' and 'antithesis' leads to a 'synthesis', which in the short term reconciles the two opposed forces, but in due course reveals tensions of its own, which will require a further synthesis. To put it another way, thoughts that appear stable show themselves not to be, and turn into their opposites before changing into more complex thoughts. Thus the thought of 'being' tends to turn into thought about 'nothing', which resolves itself in the thought of 'becoming'.

I could go on. I could mention that Kierkegaard's surname meant 'churchyard', that Baruch de Spinoza's *Ethics* is really a manual of geometry, or that Thomas Hobbes in *Leviathan* represents people as being rather like machines, bent on satisfying their cravings and in need of a powerful overlord who affords protection in return for their renouncing some of their basic freedoms. Alternatively, I could say this: philosophy is a process, rather than a product, and philosophers are, as I earlier remarked in passing, people who refresh the vocabulary of political and moral thought. In the strict etymological sense, a philosopher is a lover of wisdom, but it takes a pedant to insist on the strict etymological sense of words, and that way madness lies – a place where a 'candidate' has always to be dressed in white and 'prestige' is a feat of illusion. Philosophy is all about asking questions rather than necessarily furnishing solutions. Furthermore, it tends to come up when people are clearly under the influence of a particular philosophy – as when someone says, 'Luckily for me, I'm an existentialist.'

Five philosophical touchstones

1. The Categorical Imperative. This is associated with Kant, who writes that one should 'act only according to that maxim through which you can at the same time will that it should become a universal law'. This boils down to the idea that you should only do things that you would want to become compulsory practice. Simplified, it goes something like this: 'Do to others only whatever you would willingly have them always do to you.' In its most reduced form – 'Treat others as you would wish to be treated yourself' – this is known as the Golden Rule.

2. Occam's Razor. Named after William of Occam, a fourteenth-century thinker. The 'razor' is used to shave away superfluous arguments: what we are left with is the notion that 'entities should not be unnecessarily multiplied', or, to put it more baldly, 'the simplest explanation is the best'.

3. Buridan's Ass. This is a paradoxical situation that gets its name from a French philosopher of the fourteenth century, although it can be traced back as far as Aristotle. Essentially, an ass (a donkey, not a bottom) finds itself

between two stacks of hay that are of identical quality and size. Unable to make a rational decision about which stack it should eat, it eats neither and starves to death. It's not hard to see what lesson somebody might take from this; one argument is that anyone who, faced with two options, considers them equally appealing is not evaluating the options carefully enough.

4. The Law of Excluded Middle. All statements are either true or false; there is no middle ground between the two. This isn't the same as saying there is no middle ground between opposites such as hot and cold, but rather that a statement such as 'I am hot' is either true or false.

5. Schrödinger's Cat. A thought experiment devised by Erwin Schrödinger. A cat is in a sealed steel box. It cannot be seen. Also locked in the box are a radioactive isotope, a Geiger counter and a mechanism linking the Geiger counter to a hammer and a vial of cyanide gas. There is a 50/50 chance of the isotope decaying within an hour, and if it does so the hammer will break the vial and the cat will be killed by the cyanide. Until we look inside the box we do not know whether the isotope has decayed, and, according to quantum theory, it occupies a superposition where it is both decayed and not-decayed. This, awkwardly, means that the cat is at the same time dead and not-dead. Some readers may detect a similarity to the TV show *Deal or No Deal*.

The question of what philosophy is and does is one that comes up far, far more often than any issue to do with what a particular philosopher has thought or said. One longstanding idea is that philosophy can be consoling. It arises from the need to deal with what we might think of as life's irritations – nagging questions about, say, the value of religious belief or the proper way to sort out a dispute. The process is therapeutic. But then again, plenty of people will feel narked that the rigorous thinking of philosophers fails to achieve consensus. Philosophy arrives at few concrete findings, and reflection seems in practice to have the effect of destroying what one thought was perfectly robust knowledge. This may explain why many college philosophy graduates find the world of work hard to get on with. Their musings are enough to make one subscribe wholeheartedly to Sturgeon's Law – that 90 per cent of everything is crap.

One of the most annoying people I knew in my later teens, Calvin, had a wearyingly effective way of arguing, in which he would insist that even the most mundane statements had to be justified. So, for instance, I might say, 'Of course, Guinness in Ireland is much better than the Guinness you get in England,' and Calvin would ask, 'What's your justification for that?' There was usually some sort of justification that could be proffered, but it was apt to implode. I don't think Calvin ever needed to go any further than this ('Sunday always seems a rather sad day.' 'Can you justify that?') to win his reputation as a person of really probing intelligence. He was a Philosopher with a capital *P*, by which I mean that he was studying Philosophy but also that he thought of himself as a shrewd, calm, question-asking teaser-out of genuine knowledge and sound reasoning. He became not an explicator of Kant, but a City solicitor.

Here seems to be a good place to say something about lying. There are two reasons for doing so at this point. The first is that philosophers are greatly exercised by lying. The second, fundamental to this book: if you want to talk about things you don't really know about, you need some familiarity with the mechanics of deception, a complex behaviour requiring forethought, social intelligence, a good memory and a certain flexibility. Bluffing is not the same as lying. To begin with, people expect you to bluff from time to time, and besides, in bluffing you ignore the truth, whereas a liar remains acutely aware of the truth. One is fake: the other *false*. One has a goal in mind: the other takes pleasure in the act of deception. But both are all around you. And being good at deception, fibbing, talking bull and all the rest of it involves an ability to spot those vices in others.

Some professions demand a capacity to lie convincingly. If you are a stockbroker, a prostitute, a diplomat or a wine merchant, you will have done it plenty of times. It is a given that politicians lie, but so do chefs, estate agents, doctors and nurses. 'There's nothing wrong with you,' 'This area is really on the up,' 'It's supposed to taste like that,' 'This is an unmissable opportunity,' 'It's ready to drink now,' 'It's the biggest I've ever seen': most of us have heard this sort of thing. We are used to being confronted with hyperbole, euphemism, the deliberate omission of facts, the massaging of statistics, the suggestion that something banal is actually a mystery.

People think they know how liars behave. It is commonly imagined, for instance, that liars tend to be fidgety and will often avert their gaze from the people to whom they are speaking. A liar is also expected to touch himself (especially his face) and to appear nervous. But nervousness is not brought on only by lying, while self-touching and self-manipulation are surprisingly unreliable indicators of deception. Often we will mistakenly think someone is lying when he or she is not. People who are just socially awkward will be taken for liars, while confident deceivers will be accepted as truth-tellers.

Stereotypes of liars usually refer to what are thought of as telltale behaviours – gestures, tics, contortions and so on. It is certainly true that we find it hard to control our non-verbal behaviour. One reason for this is that we tend to have had much more practice in our use of words than we have had in our use of behaviour, and we are more aware of what we are saying than of the way we are behaving. Furthermore, whereas it is easy not to say anything, it is hard to silence our behaviour. And there are ineradicable links between our feelings and our behaviours.

It is true that when we lie we may well exhibit behaviours that indicate we are doing so: we speak at a higher pitch, pause more often and for longer, make fewer and more deliberate movements with our bodies, and maybe even fake a smile. But it is also accurate to say that someone who is keen not to be identified as a liar will try hard not to do these things. The result of this can be a forced sort of normality, which actually feels anything but normal. Liars can appear rehearsed and stilted – or they can seem unusually fluent. Their behaviour lacks spontaneity. The more complex the lie, the more this is the case. However, this poses a problem for people who are trying to identify lies.

Research suggests that very few people can successfully distinguish between truth and lies more than 60 per cent of the time. The chance of merely guessing whether someone is lying is 50 per cent, so this 60 per cent is not an impressive improvement on guesswork. Strikingly, too, research shows that the people most adept at spotting lies are not those whose jobs require them to do so – police officers and customs officials – but the people most likely to lie themselves, namely criminals.

The belief that non-verbal behaviour holds the key to establishing whether a person is telling the truth or not can divert our attention from something perhaps more valuable: what a person is saying. In practice, liars refer to themselves less than people who are telling the truth. They also make more statements that could be thought of as 'negative', expressing distaste or hostility.

There are numerous reasons why lies often go undetected. One is that the differences between a person who is lying and a person who is telling the truth can be minute. A second is that not all liars behave the same way. Additionally, the unwritten rules of politeness prevent us from actively pursuing people we suspect of lying; it is commonly considered rude to bombard a person with tightly focused questions and to insist repeatedly on details being clarified. (One of the best ways to catch out a liar, if he has concocted some sort of story, is to ask him to narrate the events in reverse order.) A final curious point is that many people are surprisingly uninterested in the truth.

Effective deception pretty obviously involves skilful acting and a degree of plausible eloquence. One also needs to have a good memory. But there is another factor: the ability to be original. Some people will dazzle a predator, as an octopus does. When an octopus is under attack, it shoots out a cloud of dark ink and propels itself to safety. Obfuscation is one of the techniques of book talk. It's not a question of being pretentious or ridiculous, but rather of appearing complex and thoughtful.

I'll be more specific now, by talking about poker. Because for everyone who has a bumper sticker saying 'I'd rather be reading Jane Austen', there must be quite a few who have the T-shirt or lapel badge that says 'Poker is life', and some of the fundamentals of poker apply nicely to the stuff we are concerned with in this book. First of all, a good player does not need good cards; the appearance of having good cards matters more. You should play the way you would play if you knew what hand your opponent was holding. Any information about what hand your opponent is holding is of value. Aggressive tactics work best against a background of being a generally tight player. Quitting while you are ahead is a sign of weakness. You shouldn't gloat when you are successful. Friendship is probably more important than winning. Finally, and crucially, good poker players don't play when they are drunk.

As for how to get a philosopher off your doorstep, here's my suggestion: pay for the pizza.

17

A SHORT HISTORY OF RATHER
LESS THAN EVERYTHING:
SCIENCE AND THE BIG IDEAS

The correct approach to playing poker, and to the very subject of this book, is scientific, inasmuch as one has to har-
vest information, process it and evaluate it. But writers on
scientific subjects, who have explained the very structures of
our existence, are casually overlooked. Experts in these fields
are considered boffins or geeks. Yet what are the most important books ever written? Not *Middlemarch* and *Ulysses*, you can
be sure. If we understand 'importance' to consist of gravity,
consequence and urgency, the sort of works that come to mind
are *Das Kapital* and *On the Origin of Species*. Yet when we are
canvassed about the books we think one ought to have read,
those most often cited are not straightforwardly useful ones full
of facts, but rather works of fiction, the fruits of the creative
imagination.

Scientists quite reasonably complain that many educated or
at any rate self-professedly educated people seem almost to
pride themselves on how little they know about physics or
chemistry. It is socially acceptable – wrongly, I might add, yet
beyond dispute – to imagine that the earth is the centre of the

universe, or to have not the first idea how blood flows around the body. To paraphrase Darwin, ignorance begets confidence far more than knowledge does. Hence the steely assurance with which ill-informed and credulous punters spew out the fustian horseshit that is Creationism and Scientology.

You are familiar with Darwin, Newton, Einstein, Freud and Stephen Hawking. But what did they write? What's in their books? I can remember as a teenager seeing on my parents' bookshelves a volume which had, I think, the title *Freud, Biologist of the Mind*. Later, a friend's father questioned my rather too casual reference to something being 'Freudian'. 'What's Freud actually all about, though?' he asked. I didn't know. 'Wasn't he a, er, biologist of the mind?' I suggested. My friend's dad looked intrigued. 'And what's that?' I hadn't given it much thought, and I admitted as much. He was jubilant: 'It's all about sex. *All* about sex. Sexual factors are the basis of human neuroses, and all your important memories tend to be sexual.' He paused, adding the word 'sex' again, just in case my friend or I had missed it the previous four times.

Freud's name is so often dropped: it is forever linked with sex, the irrational domain he called the Unconscious, the notion of the Oedipus complex, the so-called Freudian slip where – nudge, nudge – you say one thing but mean your mother. Boiled down, the legacy of Freud is the conviction that the inner life can be studied systematically, and, more popularly, a sensitivity to the power of one's inner life: dreams, undisclosed thoughts, desires, memories, repressions. A few curious addenda, though: his first scientific paper was about the testicles of eels, one of his patients was the composer Gustav Mahler (Mahler only consulted him once, but the session lasted four hours), and he was an advocate of the medical use of cocaine. Freud arrived at his basic insights as a result of reading literature – Shakespeare, Sophocles, Dostoevsky – and the case histories he wrote were literary in their novelish expansion of medical notes into skilfully plotted narratives. He chose as the epigraph to his book *The Interpretation of Dreams* some lines from Virgil's *Aeneid*, which can be translated 'If I am not able to bend the higher powers, I shall move the infernal regions.'

Instead of talking about Freud, or about Carl Gustav Jung with his conviction that the basic purpose of life is 'to kindle a light in the darkness of mere being', try talking about Jacques Lacan. Freud is widely known, and many people have at least a passing acquaintance with his main ideas. By contrast Lacan is so difficult a thinker that it is possible to pin just about anything on him. Because he's so hard to fathom, his work is sometimes reduced to a few soundbites that serve as slogans for his theories. So, 'There is no such thing as a sexual relationship,' 'The unconscious is structured like a language,' 'It is precisely because desire is articulated that it is not articulable,' 'We are practitioners of the symbolic function.' If you're going to say any of these things, you'll either need to make it very clear that the words belong inside big inverted commas, or you'll need to have had a lot to drink. But you'll make your mark.

What are the books that have changed the world?

When Melvyn Bragg set out to answer this question in his *Twelve Books That Changed the World* (2006), he decided on a group of volumes few people could claim to have read.

Darwin's *On the Origin of Species* was there, with its exposition of the principle of evolution by natural selection. (You won't find any reference to the 'survival of the fittest' in its pages – or in any of his other works. The phrase was coined by Herbert Spencer, after reading Darwin's book.) Darwin's may be the greatest story ever told, but it's a story taken for granted. A few of the other titles chosen were ones that at least a few people actually trouble to read. The King James Bible, intended to make the scriptures accessible, influenced the entire public language of morality. Adam Smith's *The Wealth of Nations* laid the foundation of modern economics, exalting the ideas of free trade, meritocracy and the beneficial effects of self-interest, and thus achieving a vision of capitalism – albeit more noble than that of many modern capitalists. Mary Wollstonecraft's *A Vindication of the Rights of Woman* promoted the education of her sex, arguing strongly against the tradition of keeping them in 'ignorance and slavish dependence'. The first folio of Shakespeare's plays, published in 1623, brought together for the first time thirty-six of the dramatist's works, and half of the plays we now consider Shakespeare's have survived to the present only because they were included in that folio.

But then there were Bragg's other choices. Isaac Newton's *Principia Mathematica* provided the basis for modern physics, rigorously explaining the principles of time and motion. Marie Stopes's *Married Love*, subtitled 'A New Contribution to the Solution of Sex Difficulties', promoted the idea that women could and should derive pleasure from sex. In 1918, the year of its publication, this was radical. *Married Love* argued that women should seek sexual satisfaction, counselled the use of birth control, and taught a generation of couples about the function of the clitoris. Seven centuries earlier, Magna Carta, a charter drawn up because of disagreements about the role of King John, established some of the basic and lasting principles of constitutional law. The rules of Association Football were agreed in 1863 by a group of public school alumni in the Freemason's Tavern in Holborn. To give a single example: 'Neither tripping nor hacking shall be allowed, and no player shall use his hands to hold or push his adversary.' William

---

Seven more books that changed the world

1. William Harvey, *De motu cordis* (1628). Promoted the idea of the circulation of blood around the human body.

2. Harriet Beecher Stowe, *Uncle Tom's Cabin* (1852). Its strong abolitionist stance fuelled furious public debate about slavery in America.

3. Rachel Carson, *Silent Spring* (1962). Focusing on the damage done by pesticides, Carson's book is credited as one of main inspirations for modern environmentalism.

4. Carl von Clausewitz, *On War* (1832). Commonly considered the greatest study of military strategy, *On War* influenced Mao Tse-tung, Hitler and Eisenhower, among others.

5. Simone de Beauvoir, *The Second Sex* (1949). Arguably the most important work of twentieth-century feminism.

6. Thomas Malthus, *Essay on the Principle of Population* (1798). A stark and original warning about the dangers of unchecked population growth.

7. Thomas Paine, *The Rights of Man* (1791). A seminal essay on the importance of human rights, equality and justice.

Wilberforce's four-hour speech in Parliament on the abolition of the slave trade, delivered on 12 May 1789 and printed in several versions soon after, was a compelling defence of the equality of mankind. The three volumes of Michael Faraday's *Experimental Researches in Electricity* illuminated the principles of electricity and magnetism. Richard Arkwright's patent specification for his spinning machine, entered in 1769, can be seen as one of the first steps towards the Industrial Revolution.

One of the points of *Twelve Books That Changed the World* is that the size of a book's influence is not the same as the size of its audience. Far more people have read *The Da Vinci Code* than have read *Principia Mathematica* – perhaps, I don't know, 10,000 times as many, even though Newton's book has been around roughly sixty times as long – but you would need to be very contrary to claim that Dan Brown's novel has done more to shape civilization.

What other books are there in this vein?

Talk about the important scientific books pretty much no one has troubled to read frequently throws up the example of Stephen Hawking's *A Brief History of Time*. One of the surprise bestsellers of the 1980s, Hawking's is a book people delight in having bought but never having opened. When they think of Hawking, they think of two things: the phenomenal commercial success of *A Brief History of Time*, and the fact that he has motor neurone disease (to be precise, amyotrophic lateral sclerosis). They may also remember the story of how 'someone told me that each equation I included in the book would halve the sales', with the result that Hawking 'resolved not to have any equations at all'. Numbers are famously offputting. (In isolation, a statistic – such as that we lose 45,000 pubic hairs in a lifetime – is amusing. Bunched together, though, figures don't read nicely.) In the end *A Brief History of Time* does contain one equation, but that is the most famous equation in the world: $E=mc^2$.

This formula, derived by Albert Einstein in 1905, requires a word of explanation. The formula shows the relationship between mass and energy. E stands for the energy of a physical system, which we measure in joules; m for mass, measured in kilograms; and c for the speed of light (roughly 186,000 miles per second). Accordingly, energy is the mass of an object multiplied by the speed of light squared: energy and mass are thus proportional and are elements of the same event. In other words, in an object of even tiny mass, a huge amount of energy is locked up. In principle, a kilogram of mass can be translated into more than 20 billion kilowatt hours of energy. This helps explain how a small portion of uranium in a nuclear bomb can be converted into enough energy to destroy a city.

Reflecting on his decision to include the equation in the book, Hawking writes, 'I hope that this will not scare off half of my potential readers.' It certainly did not scare off buyers, but readers . . . well, I'm not sure. Far fewer people have read the book than are aware of the references to it and its creator in *Family Guy*, *Donnie Darko* and *Star Trek*. In Series 7 of *The Simpsons*, when Homer Simpson inadvertently punctures the fabric of the space–time continuum, he says, 'I wish I'd read that book by that wheelchair guy.' The wish feels empty even if sincere. And in that he is not alone.

A Brief History of Time provides a picture of the universe, with a particular emphasis on the laws that govern gravity, since gravity is responsible for the universe's large-scale structure. Hawking explains how scientists' understanding of the nature of time has altered. Time begins with Big Bang, a 'singularity' of infinite heat and density. Hawking also explains what a black hole is (it's a collapsed star, which emits a small amount of radiation), and discusses at some length the elementary particles – no longer the protons and neutrons you might have learnt about in chemistry lessons, but now leptons and quarks, the latter available in six flavours.

One of the reasons for the success of Hawking's book was that it is written as accessibly as is reasonably possible for a work of its kind. You cannot, after all, write about quantum mechanics and the laws of thermodynamics without using a few fierce-looking words. There are some memorable lines – 'Isaac Newton was not a pleasant man,' a complete theory of the universe would enable us to 'know the mind of God', Einstein's general theory of relativity 'implied that the universe must have a beginning and, possibly, an end'. Some of the other information in the book would have seemed, at the time it was published, pretty strange to anyone except a clued-up mathematician or physicist. All galaxies, including ours, contain a large amount of 'dark matter', which we cannot see but know is there because of the gravitational effect it has on the orbits of stars. Space is 'curved'. Each day hundreds of thousands of stars explode somewhere in the universe. Moreover, if the stars we can see with the naked eye were the size of grains of salt, you could fit them all on a teaspoon, but if you were to include all the stars in the universe they would fill a ball over eight miles wide.

People don't sit around saying 'I'm a Hawkingian'; they just feel vaguely guilty about not knowing which star is closest to the earth. (It's the sun, of course. The next closest is Alpha Centauri C, but it would take you, using the most sophisticated spacecraft available, about 10,000 years to get there.) On the other hand, one does hear people saying 'I'm a Marxist' – and, maybe a bit more often, said with a knowing look, 'He's a *Marxist.*' Freud and Marx are the two modern thinkers whose names have become colloquial.

Marx's reputation rests on two books. The first of these is *The Communist Manifesto*, which he wrote with Friedrich Engels. Published in 1848, and said by Engels to be mainly Marx's work, it had its origins in his observation of, among other things, workers' strikes in England and the rioting of exploited Silesian weavers. The *Manifesto* begins with two big statements: 'A spectre is haunting Europe – the spectre of Communism' and 'The history of all hitherto existing society is the history of class struggles.' Some of what follows now sounds dated. Marx and Engels call for the overthrow of bourgeois values (law, morality, religion) and the establishment of a classless society in which there will be no private property and co-operation will replace competition. This now looks far less credible than it did for much of the twentieth century. But as a picture of the power of capitalism the book remains relevant, and it is more accessible than the second and by far the greater of Marx's two seminal works.

This is *Das Kapital*, in which Marx sets out what he calls a 'critique of political economy' – intended to 'reveal the economic law of motion of modern society'. He exposes the workings of capitalism: where it comes from, how it takes hold, how it develops, and how eventually it may fall.

The first volume of *Das Kapital* was published in 1867. Two further volumes were assembled by Engels from Marx's papers after his death, but this was still only half of the six-volume work that Marx had once envisaged. Casual references to *Das Kapital* suggest it is something solid and assured; in fact, it is fragmentary and bizarre, full of digressions, repetitions and wonky logic. Nevertheless, it bursts, especially in its opening volume, with fresh ideas, grounded on scientific foundations. As a prophet of socialism, Marx does not look too sharp any more, but he has shrewd things to say about globalization, which he calls the 'universal interdependence of nations', the social consequences of changes in the way goods are manufactured, the alienating effects of work, and the tendency to fetishize commodities and become their slave. It is quite normal today to recognize that one's attitudes are coloured by one's material circumstances – but the insight originates with Marx.

One of the unexpected qualities of *Das Kapital* is that it is a work of literature, not unlike a cross between a wacky scientist's ironic lecture notes and an experimental novel. Today, in an age when novels are full of noisy textbook-style information about neuroscience, microeconomics, restaurant management and a thousand other recherché things, a modern Marx would cast his theory of the economy and society as a work of fiction.

18

WHO MATTERS NOW? THE GREAT AMERICAN NOVEL AND ITS THIN BRITISH COUSIN

Try conducting a Google search for 'Great American Novel'. When I did so a little while back, the search engine returned 232,000 hits. By contrast, 'Great English Novel' returned 3,250; 'Great British Novel' 1,330; 'Great Irish Novel' 604; 'Great Scottish Novel' 231; and 'Great Welsh Novel' 77. Where others palely imitate its scope, the Great American Novel is a magical beast, a modern Holy Grail. The concept arose in the nineteenth century from a perceived need among American writers to achieve a distinct identity. The idea is this: a single book can be written that will encompass the complexity of this young, potent nation. Such a book will offer a definitive account of the American national character and experience. It will, even beyond that, seem determined to contain the whole world.

Most of the time the term is used jokingly – or at least no more than halfway between jest and earnest. It was in such a spirit that Philip Roth in 1973 published *The Great American Novel*, which exploits the mythic status of baseball, following a dire team called the Mundys (from Port Ruppert, New Jersey) through a season littered with defeats. I hardly need say that the novel is wilfully not great, containing for instance a good deal about baseball-playing midgets and a character whose surname is Stuvwxyz.

Ten other American novels with 'great' ambitions

1. Thomas Pynchon, *Gravity's Rainbow*
2. Don DeLillo, *Underworld*
3. Richard Wright, *Native Son*
4. Joseph Heller, *Catch-22*
5. Jane Smiley, *A Thousand Acres*
6. Saul Bellow, *The Adventures of Augie March*
7. Alice Walker, *The Color Purple*
8. John Updike, The 'Rabbit' quartet (*Rabbit, Run; Rabbit Redux; Rabbit is Rich; Rabbit at Rest*)
9. Jonathan Franzen, *The Corrections*
10. Richard Ford, *Independence Day*

But which is *the* great American novel? Ask an expert – professional, or self-appointed – and claims will be made for *Huckleberry Finn*, *The Great Gatsby* and *Moby-Dick*. Sometimes the terrain is deliberately narrowed. The best American novel since the Second World War could be Ralph Ellison's *Invisible Man* or Toni Morrison's *Beloved*, the best of the 1980s *Beloved* or Cormac McCarthy's *Blood Meridian*. Arguments on this theme are unanswerable. You can even claim, without sounding ridiculous, that the Great American Novel is not a novel at all. Maybe it's *The Sopranos* or *Six Feet Under*. Maybe it's the collected works of Bob Dylan. The debate can be seen as a symptom of cultural insecurity, but what it really points up is the need for an inspiring national myth.

There is, simultaneously, an anxiety that novels should offer a sort of social instruction – or perhaps the true anxiety is about their failure to do so, their loss of ground to other media. Recovering the past is a recurrent concern, as is the resonance of past events in the present. Words to bandy about are *disruption*, *narcissism*, *subversion* and *scepticism* (or their adjectival forms). Try, however, not to mention *postmodernism*, a word that will only make you look like a poseur. You might talk of the 'perils of prosperity', the 'absurd hero', 'passionate doubts', 'radical soap opera', the 'loss of self' and 'speaking out' – all formulae nabbed from the titles of books not many people will have read.

Over the past decade, one novelist has been canonized as the pre-eminent American writer of our time. No longer footling around with characters called things like Stuvwxyz, it's Philip Roth. In a series of books, beginning with *Sabbath's Theater* in 1995, Roth has cemented a position as the age's finest, angriest chronicler of the lives of men. His writing is antagonistic, playful, vicious, fast-moving, serious, rude. When Mickey Sabbath declares his ambition is 'to affront and affront and affront till there was no one on earth unaffronted' he sounds, in common with so many of Roth's characters, very much like his creator. In the manner of his creation Nathan Zuckerman, Roth can appear to be 'plundering his own history like a thief'. Some of Roth's novels even contain a character called Philip Roth; one, *Operation Shylock*, contains two of them.

There are other strands in Roth's work: the idea that fear can bring about actions that tear the very heart out of society and democracy, a sense that personality is something like a glove and can be put on or casually cast aside, the comedy of failure, the notion that Jewishness is a gift and an affliction, the awareness that fictional characters have a habit of breaking free from the printed page. Roth's fiction has a deliberately puerile quality – his most famous novel remains *Portnoy's Complaint* (1969), which is in part a hymn to masturbation – and one of the frequent British objections to much American fiction is this puerility. But, to quote a writer Roth evidently admires, the Pole Witold Gombrowicz, 'If you are repelled by immaturity, it is because you are immature.' For both Gombrowicz and Roth, immaturity seems true and real, in a way that its alternative does not.

Roth is actually held in high regard by British readers, but he is also viewed with suspicion – as an anti-Semite and a misogynist, or, less awkwardly but still damningly, as a joyless writer or a clever clogs hung up on narrative ploys and the absurd, on scatological stuff and on himself. He is seen as being too self-consciously literary, a writer lost in his own imagined universe. In short, his ambition is mistrusted.

How is Britain different?

British distaste for 'big' American novels is palpable. Really it is part of a distaste for the bigness of America. Insisting that American writers disregard their country's bigness and write instead the Stateside equivalent of 'Death in Leamington' is a bit like expecting Michelangelo to pop round and paint your bathroom ceiling. Of course, no one strenuously insists on this; it is something that happens by implication. For British fiction tends to be parochial, even when on the surface it is international. (Saying so is a great way to start an argument. Watch the sparks – and the counterexamples – fly.) Even meaty-looking books are thin, and the big game they promise to hunt turns out to be small, warm, flat beer.

Since the 1970s, when it seemed to move sharply away from an unworldly insularity, British fiction has been expected to focus on other times and, to a lesser degree, other places. To be alive is to be haunted. Yet the affair with abroad never quite escapes a soapy sort of provincialism, and bound up with this is a persistent anxiety about what it means to be British. Is it a privilege or a burden, something to cherish or forget (or perhaps deny or neglect)? There is also an anxiety about 'reality', which somehow seems less plausible, stable and truthful than the imaginary and the fantastic.

In Britain, public debate about fiction is provoked by prizes. Book clubs and reading groups play significant parts, but the most visible and audible discussions are stimulated by awards – notably the Booker Prize (now officially the Man Booker Prize), which has run for the past forty years. The Booker is open to authors of fiction, writing in English, who are citizens of the Commonwealth or the Republic of Ireland; its winners have included the Australian Peter Carey, the South African J. M. Coetzee and the Indo-Trinidadian V. S. Naipaul. The prize is also an opportunity to take the temperature of British letters. Who's hot, and who's not? There are writers who perennially interest the judges, such as Margaret Atwood (a Canadian), and many others who perennially do not.

The names on people's lips vary from season to season, but a quick tour of some of the regulars of the past decade may be in order. Ian McEwan, a staple of middle-class chat, once produced macabre short stories, but now specializes in rather more coolly disturbing novels, and is particularly concerned with the way the character and behaviour of adults is linked to the traumas of their childhood. Booker-garlanded Alan Hollinghurst writes with exquisite poise about the lives of gay men; behind the stories of social and sexual acrobatics and sophisticated repartee are the shadowy presences of politics and history. Booker-overlooked Martin Amis is a contemptuous moralist with a gift – sometimes too obtrusive – for sparky prose. Zadie Smith highlights one of her persistent interests in the epigraph of her first novel, *White Teeth* – 'What's past is prologue' – and thus usefully suggests the way her characters' awareness of their present is framed by history. David Mitchell is a skilful ventriloquist who maps the unseen connections between apparently unrelated episodes. Ali Smith is a mesmerist who enjoys dark puns and unresolved endings.

The novels of Jeanette Winterson are lyrical and erotically charged, usually have androgynous main characters, and manage to be both experimental and almost Biblical in their moral conviction. Graham Swift writes with sparse clarity about friendships, marriages, death and sex, creating mystery out of the ordinary, and almost always avoiding a linear account of events. Will Self is a mordantly intelligent and misanthropic satirist, who is nonetheless oddly lugubrious. Iain Sinclair is a sort of footsore shaman whose books are blistered with arcane information and loopy preoccupations. J. G. Ballard investigates the dark corners of the modern psyche and the modern city in an unsettling manner that might put one in mind of a surrealist engineering student. Doris Lessing, interest in whom was recently revitalized by the award of the Nobel Prize for

Literature, is a feminist sceptical of such labels, whose work has been informed, in succession, by communism, radical psychiatry and Islamic mysticism. Statements of this kind are, of course, superficial and blurby, and this brisk list misses all kinds of people out, but even book-length surveys of the field seem hopelessly partial, in both senses of that word.

The biggest name to conjure with is that of Salman Rushdie, and the perennial question regarding Rushdie is 'What's all the fuss about?' Rushdie is globally famous on account of the violent outrage caused by his fourth novel, *The Satanic Verses*, which was published in the autumn of 1988. Its title refers to two verses known to Muslims as the *gharaniq* verses or 'the story of the cranes'. These lines were supposedly spoken by Muhammad while reciting the Qur'an, and later retracted; in them he appears to endorse divinities other than Allah. Rushdie's novel uses this episode to question the validity of divine revelation. While *The Satanic Verses* is essentially about the immigrant experience in Britain – its two main characters are Indian actors working in England – it caused offence to Muslims because of its apparent suggestion that the Qur'an was Satanic, as well as through other details that were perceived as blasphemous. A trio of examples: a disastrous pilgrimage is led by a girl called Ayesha, which was the name of one of Muhammad's wives; a character considered to represent Muhammad is shown visiting brothels; and Mecca is depicted as Jahilia, a city built on sand. The book was publicly burnt in Bolton and Bradford, and in February 1989 Iran's Supreme Leader, Ayatollah Khomeini, called on Muslims to kill all those involved with the novel's publication. The call was taken seriously. To give just two instances, the book's Japanese translator, Hitoshi Igarashi, was murdered, and the offices of a New York newspaper which defended its publication were firebombed.

The Satanic Verses, as both novel and phenomenon, shows reality being overtaken by the imaginary and the barely imaginable, at the same time as the imaginary falls victim to the real, and it is with this kind of exchange in mind that Rushdie suggests in one of his essays that we need books that 'draw new and better maps of reality'. The statement reflects his interest in a subject now out of fashion but still noteworthy: magic realism. The form's best-known English-language practitioner, Rushdie has defined it as the 'commingling of the improbable and the mundane'. Two or more worlds rub against each other. The real is presented magically: magic is presented realistically. The effect is that both categories are called into question, and the boundary between them is unsettled.

In his best novel, *Midnight's Children*, Rushdie documents sixty years in the history of the countries now called India, Pakistan and Bangladesh, in a style that blends autobiography, history and elements of the sort of tales included in the *Arabian Nights*. The children of the book's title are the 581 who survive of the 1,001 born in the first hour of 15 August 1947, the day India became independent from British rule. The unreliable narrator, Saleem Sinai, is one of these. He explains that these children 'can be seen as the last throw of everything antiquated . . . in our myth-ridden nation' or as 'the true hope of freedom, which is now forever extinguished'. Each of the children has a vision of India, and yet over the course of the book each either dies or becomes impotent, suggesting the disintegration of their country.

A discernible influence on the flamboyant fantasies of *Midnight's Children* is the Colombian novelist Gabriel García

Márquez (pronounced *mar-kes*, with the stress on the first syllable), and from Márquez, as from Rushdie, one gleans a sense that
the magic of magic realism is no mere flight of fancy, but instead
exists to serve political ends. What looks like an evasion of political content is actually a flank attack on politics. Thus in
Márquez's most celebrated novel, *One Hundred Years of Solitude*,
rain falls for years on end and there is an epidemic of insomnia,
while clouds of yellow butterflies symbolize forbidden love, and
ghosts make friends with the people who sent them into the
afterlife; but Márquez also offers a fictionalized account of a
strike by some banana workers in the Colombian coastal town
of Ciénaga in 1928. The details of this real event are no less
extraordinary than the obviously magical parts of the novel. The
authorities and the United Fruit Company crushed the workers'
protest in the most brutal fashion: the army came in and massa-
cred the strikers. The number of deaths is not officially known
(the strike leaders claimed 1,500), because the military regime
insisted that the incident did not take place. In the novel the only
adult witness to survive is José Arcadio Segundo, a union activist.
His recollection of events is useless, because no one will corrob-
orate it. Márquez draws attention to a real event that has been
effaced from history because of a conspiracy of silence, and suggests the questionable reliability of history in general.

The Colombian has found a large audience outside the
Spanish-speaking world, especially in English. But generally in
Britain and America there is a selective appreciation of literature not written in the native language. The British media,
largely impervious to anything not puffed by news agencies and
PR companies, seldom pick up on foreign evidence of literary
achievement, and, thus blinkered, they have over the past few

decades announced and lamented the demise of the novel. It is often alleged that non-fiction has claimed the intellectual high ground from fiction. In a not unrelated move, it is said that science has claimed the intellectual high ground from the arts.

Ten novels not written in English that are anxiously – or grudgingly – revered by novelists who do write in English.

1. Günter Grass, *The Tin Drum* (German)
2. Michel Houellebecq, *Atomised* (French)
3. Umberto Eco, *Foucault's Pendulum* (Italian)
4. José Saramago, *The Year of the Death of Ricardo Reis* (Portuguese)
5. Haruki Murakami, *The Wind-Up Bird Chronicle* (Japanese)
6. Ngugi wa Thiong'o, *Wizard of the Crow* (Gikuyu)
7. Naguib Mahfouz, *The Cairo Trilogy*, especially *Palace Walk* (Arabic)
8. Milan Kundera, *The Joke* (Czech)
9. Roberto Bolaño, *The Savage Detectives* (Spanish)
10. Orhan Pamuk, *My Name Is Red* (Turkish)

This is classic dinner-party territory. 'Oh, I gave up on novels a while back. Now I read mainly business books. And Eastern philosophy.' But the greatest hazard of the dinner table, short of sashimi-ing your index finger, is finding yourself next to an author. I possess an old cartoon depicting two people exchanging chitchat at a social function. One says to the other, 'I'm writing a novel', which is met with the response 'Neither am I'. Someone who holds forth about his work in progress is usually not getting much done on it. Productive authors, on the other hand, are discreet about their productivity. Literary biographies are full of information about all that happens in authors' lives – except the gritty business of producing the words that made them famous. This is because the practice of writing is inscrutable, and also because it is not interesting *per se*. In ordinary social situations, people who are voluble about their writing quickly become bores. And someone you know to be a writer, if apparently reluctant to divulge the minute details of her craft, is conserving her creativity.

When dealing with authors, remember they are a bit like spiders: more scared of you than you are of them. It is a very strange author who would rather talk about his or her writing than *be* writing. But there are situations in which authors are required to violate this principle. They must make a living, and this involves all manner of mutually awkward interactions with their public. On such occasions – at readings and other 'author events' – there seems to be an unwritten rule, in my summary of which I can hardly help sounding like a cheap version of Oscar Wilde: for an author on parade, the only thing worse than being asked questions is not being asked questions.

I once went to a reading by the novelist Vikram Seth. (His surname, by the way, rhymes not with *death*, but with *late*, and the first rhyme of his verse novel *The Golden Gate* – dubbed the Great Californian Novel by Gore Vidal – thus occurs on the jacket.) At the end he took questions. I asked a number, all of them about Seth's *A Suitable Boy*, which had been published a couple of years before. My questions drew careful, thoughtful responses. But I had not read the book. I later did, and one of my main memories of it is that it contains a surprising amount about shoe manufacture. At the time of the reading, I had little to work with. Yet I had read enough *about* Vikram Seth to be able to sound authoritative.

The questions asked in such a situation need either to be large – 'What is the role of the novelist today?', 'Where do you get your ideas?' – or closely focused. The nightmare question, for all involved, is one that aspires to be exact but manages only to be woolly. At a talk by Martin Amis which I attended several years ago, a member of the audience wondered, 'I'm interested in an image in one of your books. Can you remember it? You describe one character "getting to the bottom" of another's personality. Do you remember that image?' Amis was admirably generous in the face of this fatuity, trying to locate the image in one of his novels. The rest of the audience chewed their fists. The image was so commonplace that it surely warranted neither recall not exploration. Was the piss being taken? No. This was, it seemed, a simple case of someone who had actually read a particular book doing a good impression of someone who had never read *any* book.

It is in the context of discussions about contemporary writers and their works that we are most likely to come across fakery. These writers, many of them only very briefly in the full flush of vogue, are a gift to the chancer, who can download ready-made opinions of them in an instant, knowing that almost no one will be able to contest these views. But this is widely recognized – those hurried words of praise for a fashionable new book ring hollow, whether securely grounded or not – and it is in dealing with the contemporary that one can achieve a perverse victory by saying, 'I don't know.' When we are presented with an opportunity to talk about books we haven't read, sometimes we benefit most from exhibiting our integrity. Deciding whether to do so involves, of course, the social game theory to which I referred in my opening chapter.

———

What to say at a book group

Back in my opening chapter I mentioned *The Jane Austen Book Club*, and now I've emphasized the role of book clubs and reading groups in fostering a more general discussion of literary taste.

Anyone serious about participating in a book group is going to want to read most of the books chosen for discussion. But many people who belong to such groups have been known now and then to turn up without having done their homework. They tend to get away with it.

One of the main reasons for this is that, with rare exceptions, book groups are designed to be unintimidating. They often have a therapeutic aspect; people are inspired by their reading to talk openly about their problems. Consequently it's a very bad idea to go into a meeting with all guns blazing. Your approach should instead be considered, gentle and compassionate. Rumbling people and exposing their weaknesses and oversights is not on the agenda.

Engage with the opinions that emerge. Feel free to talk about your own neuroses – preferably some that you've made up for the occasion. And as for covering up your ignorance, there is, paradoxically, no better way to do this than by volunteering to lead the group.

———

19

POPULAR BOOKS: IS THERE ANY EXCUSE?

The disdain is audible. I am having dinner with friends and I mention that I am reading Rupert Everett's autobiography. 'What are you reading *that* for?' asks the soigné MBA sitting opposite me. I say, rather feebly, that it is gossipy, accessible, funny, but I know this is not enough. I obviously ought to be reading something more like what he is reading – which transpires to be a book about the ethics of healthcare management.

Most people who read are happy at least from time to time to read something that's not a cast-iron classic. Many do a deal with themselves: 'I can read the new John Grisham if I read *To the Lighthouse* first.' I am content to say I am such a person. I may have read all Shakespeare's plays, the more than 2,000 pages of Dr Johnson's *Dictionary* and all of Samuel Pepys's diaries, but I've also found time to enjoy Armistead Maupin's *Tales of the City*, Stephen King and the autobiography of an obscure American tennis player called Vince Spadea, and I am more than happy to leaf through a free magazine on the loo.

I'm not suggesting that *Tales of the City* and *Middlemarch* have equal merit. But then again, there is too much snobbery about so-called 'genre' writing: thrillers, science fiction and fantasy, historical novels, children's books. One of the more absurd phenomena of bookselling is the 'Black Interest' section some shops have, as if Toni Morrison, Ralph Ellison and Ngugi wa Thiong'o are not of interest to anyone who might not seek out this particular niche. There is a lot of piffle published in all the 'genre' areas, but there is also a good deal of ordure that gets dignified as 'literary fiction'. I rather like the comment made by Terry Pratchett, a popular author of satirical fantasy novels that have consistently failed to interest the literary establishment: 'I think about the literary world like I think about Tibet. It's quite interesting, it's a long way away from me and it's sure as hell they're never going to make me Dalai Lama.'

For all the snootiness about Terry Pratchett and countless other authors like him who are casually dismissed, popular books are conversational staples. While there may be a stigma attached to having read them (or to admitting to having read them), there is also a certain awkwardness that results from not having read them. As a friend's wife once said to me over a plate of crispy duck, 'You haven't read Dave Pelzer? How can you say you've lived?' It is impossible to keep abreast of even the latest prizewinners and Richard & Judy selections, let alone the acres of kitsch, true confessions, romantic novels, hackneyed thrillers and the whole gamut of 'misery' books.

Remember, then, that a bestseller chimes with a particular cultural moment. At any other point, it would barely have worked. (I'm not including here perennial successes, such as the predictable and unexciting popularity of *The Highway Code*.) Remove a bestseller from its cultural moment, and it looks and sounds quite wrong. Its success is to do with what the Greeks called *kairos*, 'the right time' – the opportune moment at which something special can happen. The award of a prestigious prize, a film adaptation or an ill-tempered spat in the press may create this right time. Generally, hype cannot. The biggest successes are achieved through word of mouth, when a book – *The Kite Runner* or *Captain Corelli's Mandolin* – is recommended person to person or by other means that appear more 'honest' than conventional marketing. 'Honest' belongs in queasy inverted commas because word of mouth has become something that can be contrived through viral advertising and targeting influential chatterers.

As we know, Dan Brown's *The Da Vinci Code* prospered to an astonishing degree through word-of-mouth endorsements, and it seemed to engage deeply with a particular moment. I can remember in the winter of 2005, as I walked along the aisle on a flight from Buenos Aires to El Calafate, counting eight passengers reading *El Código Da Vinci*, and only one other perusing something that wasn't a magazine or a Sudoku puzzle collection. *The Da Vinci Code* not only works as a thriller – every chapter ends on a cliff-hanger, and there are a lot of chapters – but also manages to make its readers feel intelligent as they (okay, we) piece together the plot's mysteries. Yet this is true of many thrillers. The peculiar success of *The Da Vinci Code* owes a great deal, I am sure, to its having been published in April 2003. Its blend of conspiracy story, revisionist history and paranoid speculation appealed to a post-9/11 society intent on finding sinister and often outlandish explanations for the world's ills. On his website Brown posed the rhetorical question 'How historically accurate is history itself?' *The Da Vinci Code* appealed especially to people eager to believe that the history they had been fed in school and by the mass media – including the very recent history – was a tissue of elaborate fictions designed to mask an unpalatable truth.

Popular fiction plays on the anxieties and manias of the moment, and also on its conventions. This is why it is so ephemeral. As John Sutherland has suggested, 'Imagine Bridget Jones in a utility dress, and rayon stockings, in 1948 ("2 units of brown ale. Bad. 6 Willy Woodbines. v.gd.").' If you don't have a clue about *Bridget Jones's Diary*, suffice it to say that Helen Fielding's novel – originally a weekly column in the *Independent* – is a loose modernization of *Pride and Prejudice*, revolving around the mundane misadventures of a thirty-three-year-old singleton who is desperate to stop smoking, lose weight and (possibly) find love. This information may well be superfluous; Sutherland reckons Bridget is 'the most famous heroine since Jane Eyre'. But will *Bridget Jones's Diary* be read in 2030? Maybe, thanks to the connection with Austen. But probably not. For the most part the hot titles of the moment are tomorrow's – or at any rate the next decade's – charity-shop stock.

Five popular contemporary novelists it's 'okay' to like

1. Philip Pullman
2. Donna Leon
3. James Ellroy
4. John Le Carré
5. Ian Rankin

Confronted, then, by someone who is trumpeting the virtues of the latest indispensable publication – be it a 'brilliant' novel or a 'riveting' autobiography – you can safely digress into the curmudgeon's territory, pointing out that this sort of success is transient. Reflecting on his experiences working in a bookshop, George Orwell was able to see both that there is a massive gulf between people's real tastes and their pretended ones, and that being around large quantities of books is far from invigorating or ennobling. En masse, books testify to the fleeting nature of fame and reputation.

What do these names mean to you? Marie Corelli. Hall Caine. Warwick Deeping. Nat Gould. Ethel M. Dell. All hugely successful writers from the first part of the twentieth century, yet who reads them now? Who even knows what they wrote? For a more recent example, try Dennis Wheatley, whose fifty novels each sold about a million copies in Britain.

Orwell's friend the critic Cyril Connolly, now a largely forgotten figure, published in 1938 a long essay called *Enemies of Promise*, in which he set out to identify the qualities that enable a book to last – that is, stay in print, and stay significant – for ten years. 'Literature', states Connolly, 'is the art of writing something that will be read twice.' That which is read only once, he argues, cannot claim to rise above the level of journalism. 'Contemporary books do not keep,' he says, before more sharply observing that what makes books sell is the 'chemical combination of illusion with disillusion'. Up-to-dateness is confused with originality, and books prosper because they seem more timely – more connected to issues currently 'in the air' – than anything previously available. The up-to-date is extravagantly praised for being up to date, and nothing, as Connolly points out, kills literary reputation quite like this inflation. Confronted with the latest must-read book, brandished by its readers like a fifth gospel, feel no shame about not owning it, not knowing it. Instead, ask whether it will stand even Connolly's modest test. Will it live longer than your dog or cat? Will its fame even outlive the yoghurt in the fridge?

How to fend off a drinks-party poseur

The drinks-party poseur is probably someone you hope never to encounter again, so you can play a high-risk game. One strategy is to intimidate him or her (but probably *him*) with offhand quotations. Voltaire's 'A witty saying proves nothing'; Dorothy Parker's 'This is not a novel to be tossed aside lightly. It should be thrown with force'; that sort of line.

You can also play 'name tennis': if the person to whom you are talking insists on namedropping, volley those dropped names right back. A stealthier approach is to make none of the running; you simply respond with careful scepticism to everything that is said.

Typically, the drinks-party poseur knows no more than you do. To quote Dorothy Parker again – from an occasion when she was invited to use the word 'horticulture' correctly in a sentence – 'You can lead a horticulture, but you can't make her think.'

20

AND SO, WITH ONE EYE ON THE
EXIT . . .

There is a sketch by the American comedian Bill Hicks, in which he recalls going to a Waffle House in Nashville and being asked by the waitress, 'What you readin' for?' Not 'What are you reading?', but 'Why?' Hicks, of course, has his answer: 'I guess I read for a lot of reasons, and the main one is so I don't end up being a fuckin' waffle waitress.'

People who read often come up against a version of the waitress's question: 'What are you reading *that* for?' The implication is that they ought to be reading something more worthwhile, like a history of democracy or a car-repair manual. The mistake here is the assumption that we must read to glean information. We can read for this purpose, but there are other ends attainable. The thirst for particulars may be satisfied by imaginative writing as much as by works of fact, and this thirst is only one type of readerly necessity.

Often we read to enrich our sense of the freedoms and possibilities of existence. We are liberated by our reading. More subtly, it has the potential to extend our understanding of our own minds. We may read to test our morals – to put them to the test, that is, or to stretch them out and build them up. Our ethical sense can be engaged and refined. Moreover, we get to sample experiences we could never otherwise taste. We can be Scarlett O'Hara, bent on making everyone who's been mean to us pea-green with envy; Shakespeare's Romeo – handsome, sleepless and witty; Philip Marlowe, sleuthing philosophically, necking bourbon and smoking Camels; an adventurous orphan (Frodo Baggins, Huckleberry Finn, or even Hannibal Lecter); autistic Christopher in *The Curious Incident of the Dog in the Night-Time*, curling up in a ball to protect ourselves from a surfeit of information; or the almost self-destructively maternal heroine of Toni Morrison's *Beloved*. We meet people we would not meet anywhere else. Literature, you could say, adds to reality. It also keeps the tools of thought sharp. When reading has died, our identities will have died too.

Of course, when I sit down to read, I don't think in such terms. I certainly don't say to myself, '*Yes!* My ethical sense is about to be engaged.' I read because it gives me pleasure. But pleasure is always haunted by the suspicion that there are other things one could be doing. The reader is aware that choosing one book means deferring every other.

By the same token, there are authors and books I have not dealt with in these pages whom I might easily have included and whom, I worry, I ought to have included: Chekhov, Goethe (pronounced *gurr-tuh*, almost as though to rhyme with *hurter*), *The Epic of Gilgamesh*, the classics of Sanskrit literature such as the *Mahabharata*, Cao Xueqin's *The Story of the Stone*, William Faulkner, *Paradise Lost*, Joseph Conrad, the porno-sophical musings of Katie Price. I might have reflected on how to talk about plays you haven't read (or seen): Samuel Beckett,

Arthur Miller, Harold Pinter, Tom Stoppard; or, looking further back, Ibsen, Molière, Aristophanes. I might have talked more about poets, whom Shelley magnificently called 'the unacknowledged legislators of the world'. I might have said something about the short story, the masters of which include Henry James, D. H. Lawrence, Chekhov, Guy de Maupassant and Katherine Mansfield. But no one has read everything, and no one has seen everything, so you don't need to be able to pretend that you have done so.

Half-a-dozen literary references that have become staples of everyday speech

1. *A Faustian pact* (as mentioned in the chapter on Tolstoy and Dostoevsky). Faust, the hero of several works including Christopher Marlowe's play Dr Faustus and a 'closet drama' by Goethe, sells his soul to the Devil in return for a life of pleasure and knowledge. To a modern audience, Faust symbolizes the dangers of man's hunger for experience. A Faustian pact is a bargain that offers immediate rewards but threatens ultimate ruin.

2. *The man from Porlock.* Samuel Taylor Coleridge claimed to have visualized the whole of his poem 'Kubla Khan' in a dream (probably induced by opium). Once he woke up, he busily set about writing it down, but was interrupted after fifty-four lines by a 'person on business from Porlock' (Porlock is a village on the edge of Exmoor in Somerset). The man from Porlock is now proverbial, a figure who disturbs one's creative thought processes.

3. *Frankenstein's monster*. In popular culture, this so-called monster is a symbol of science gone mad. In Mary Shelley's original novel, though, the monster is described as a 'creature', eight feet tall but sensitive and intelligent. A common mistake is to think that Frankenstein is the name not of this wretched being's intellectually curious creator, but of the creature itself.

4. *The madwoman in the attic*. In *Jane Eyre*, Jane's lover Rochester has a secret wife, Bertha, who is insane and is locked away in an attic. The image of the supposedly deranged woman kept out of sight has been adopted by feminists – notably in a book entitled *The Madwoman in the Attic* by Sandra Gilbert and Susan Gubar – as a way of summing up the nineteenth-century suppression of women's identities. In this context madness is a metaphor for female rebelliousness.

5. *The picture of Dorian Gray*. In Oscar Wilde's only published novel, Dorian is a beautiful young man who is plunged into a life of decadence. He is painted by Basil Hallward, an artist. The picture of Dorian is his masterpiece. Dorian, worried that the beauty captured in Hallward's painting will fade, wishes that, rather than growing old, the painting could grow old instead. The wish is fulfilled, and, as Dorian becomes ever more depraved, his image in the picture grows ever more hideous. In doing so, it torments him. Dorian embodies the hypocrisy of the affluent middle class, while the picture suggests the transformative power of art.

6. *The Byronic hero*. A flawed, often lawless but impressive and ambitious character, who creates his own moral code, frequently found in the writings of Lord Byron and

exemplified by him personally. Byron's one-time lover Lady Caroline Lamb considered him 'mad, bad and dangerous to know'. Examples beyond Byron's works include the Terminator and Angel in *Buffy the Vampire Slayer*.

In my own sneaky way, I have, I'd like to think, suggested that there are reasons to read the books I've mentioned in these pages. But whether you read them or not, there are a few more strategies you can adopt in order to talk successfully about books.

If you are determined to succeed, you would do well to cultivate an at least faintly absurd persona. You can present yourself as the European obscurantist (you only read literature written east of the Alps), the iconoclast (nothing is sacred, and your default setting is to be scathing about all works of art, especially those that threaten to give other people pleasure), or – a particular favourite of mine – the unproductive poet, a tortured and pathetic soul who describes himself as a writer, even on his passport, yet never actually writes anything and spends most of his time stringing along a selection of dewy-eyed and infuriatingly good-looking young acolytes, each of whom hopes to be the inspiration for his as yet uncontemplated masterpiece.

Another option is to be an antiquarian, who rubbishes anything new, insisting that there is infinitely more merit in Tobias Smollett (whom no one under fifty has read) than in anything written since 1940. In general, it can be very useful to claim a deep but nuanced enthusiasm for someone obscure and out of fashion yet actually quite good, like Ivy Compton-Burnett or

Patrick Hamilton, or a readable but not well-known author from a country most people can picture only sketchily, such as the Czech novelist Bohumil Hrabal, the Nicaraguan poet Rubén Darío, or Tarjei Vesaas, whose beautiful novel *The Ice Palace* is known to pretty much every Norwegian, but to very few people beyond Norway. While it is handy to have opinions about the books everyone else has read, it can be even better to have opinions about books practically no one else has read – and about which therefore no one is qualified to argue with you.

Curiously, it will also be taken as a mark of wise open-mindedness to enjoy very publicly certain things that might be regarded as 'low grade': James Bond escapades, bodice-ripper romances, Tintin, one of the popular series of children's books (better Lemony Snicket than Harry Potter), or the graphic novels of Daniel Clowes. Your cherishing the 'low' will be seen as evidence that you are not a snob, in the same way that public intellectuals often make a big deal of how much they relish supposedly humdrum or philistine pursuits: watching football, playing *Grand Theft Auto*, eating breakfast in grubby cafés.

Book reviewers – an admittedly small constituency – know all about this sort of thing. Typically, a book reviewer will manage to give out the impression that he or she would rather be doing something else: watching the snooker, having another gin and tonic, getting a foot massage, or mowing the lawn. Yet this is always balanced by the impression that he or she has grappled with whatever is currently under consideration, no matter how dire. Often one has the sense of a loftily judicious soul trying terribly hard to like something before at length despairing of doing so and unwillingly giving space to a few words of spectacularly caustic comment.

Reviewers are, for the most part, culturally literate types who know that their cultural literacy makes it possible for them to get away with shoddy practices. Everyone who reviews books has some sort of code of honour. Typically, it is less than majestic ('Never review books by my friends. Always read the first 100 pages. Don't sell the proof copy on eBay'), but even reviewers with real integrity deviate from their rules. Oscar Wilde is supposed to have set the standard for the swindlers, saying, 'I never read a book I must review; it prejudices you so,' although the witticism in fact deserves to be credited to a less well-known figure, Sydney Smith. In any case, the German scientist Georg Christoph Lichtenberg had beaten both men to it. In the 1780s Lichtenberg wrote in his notebook (or 'waste book', as he called it), 'Among the greatest discoveries human reason has made in recent times is, in my opinion, the art of reviewing books without having read them.'

Taking note of book reviews – not reading them closely, but just skimming them – is a reliable way of keeping abreast of what's hot and what's not: the liberally applauded new novel about suburban vices, the Vietnam War or a Victorian pickpocket; the deeply researched tome unfurling the life of some obscure architect, eighteenth-century aristocrat or deaf-mute forger in Renaissance Perugia; the history of alphabets, the coffee bean or the turbot; the scandalously readable blockbuster set in the Pentagon, a post-apocalyptic wasteland or a Swiss finishing school; the execrable memoirs of a pop star or politico, littered with vengeful non-sequiturs; the jejune narrative of the adventures of a Wisconsin fur-trapper or the discovery of the planet Neptune. Reviewers, whether scrupulous or not, are adept at summarizing 400 pages in forty words.

Actually, as a rule, one can say that the degree of a critic's real engagement with a book and its subject is inversely proportional to his or her willingness to distil it down to a few gaudy soundbites. You can read a 3,000-word review in a literary journal and be unsure at its end of the virtues and vices of the book in question, or even of what the book is about. But a 150-word squib will tell you everything you need to know.

Five remarkable ways to end a novel

1. 'Two gin-scented tears trickled down the sides of his nose. But it was all right, everything was all right, the struggle was finished. He had won the victory over himself. He loved Big Brother' (George Orwell, *1984*)
2. 'She gloried in being a sailor's wife, but she must pay the tax of quick alarm for belonging to that profession which is, if possible, more distinguished in its domestic virtues than in its national importance' (Jane Austen, *Persuasion*)
3. 'But I reckon I got to light out for the Territory ahead of the rest, because Aunt Sally she's going to adopt me and sivilize me, and I can't stand it. I been there before' (Mark Twain, *The Adventures of Huckleberry Finn*)
4. 'So we beat on, boats against the current, borne back ceaselessly into the past' (F. Scott Fitzgerald, *The Great Gatsby*)
5. 'Yukiko's diarrhoea persisted through the twenty-sixth, and was a problem on the train to Tokyo' (Junichiro Tanizaki, *The Makioka Sisters*)

Reviewers are acutely conscious of the need to assert what I've called their cultural literacy. They often do this by dropping names. A freshly minted novel chronicling the history of a Ukrainian shtetl may draw comparison with the works of Taras Shevchenko, Isaac Babel and Isaac Bashevis Singer. Insisting on these parallels does less to reassure readers – 'Who the hell are these people?' – than it does to reinforce their awareness of the critic's expertise. People who write about books are all known to fake it – to profess, for instance, a rich knowledge of an author's back catalogue, gleaned in half an hour from Wikipedia and a handful of other more or less reliable resources. In this book, by the way, I am naughty enough to write (once) about a book I have not read, and there a couple of others I have not finished. I'll leave you to guess which they are.

There are a few authors truly beloved of hardcore fakers, on the grounds that quite a lot of people have a vague notion of what their books are like without knowing them in any detail. Kafka is a perennial favourite; the adjective 'Kafkaesque', which essentially conveys the idea of sinister and inexplicable complexity, can be applied to the surreal, disorientating hazards of pretty much any country's bureaucracy or judicial system, and seems especially well suited to the political distortions of North Korea, extraordinary rendition, or the trials of booking a table at a fashionable restaurant.

For those looking to achieve maximum effect, Jorge Luis Borges (whose surname is pronounced *bore-hess* with a rolled *r*) is even better than Kafka. The Argentine is celebrated chiefly for his short works of fiction, in which labyrinths, mirrors, circularity and infinity are recurrent concerns, as is the very business of writing – the devices and philosophy of storytelling. In his books one comes across a city where people's social positions are determined by lottery; a library that contains every book ever written, along with every book that might be written; and a language that has no nouns and consists mostly of Jenga stacks of adjectives. Borges is also an addict of useless erudition. Anything complicated, tricksy, self-aware or tinged with fantasy can be described as 'Borgesian': it may be a pretentious diagnosis, but it's a sexy one. You will rarely come across anyone qualified to challenge you on this point, and if you are unfortunate enough to do so you can simply allow the ensuing dispute to become Borgesian – which is to say, full of riddles and polymathic coquetry.

But Borges is also exemplary: he read whatever he liked, and read widely, always with enjoyment uppermost in his mind. His literary enthusiasms were quirky and patchy. According to Alberto Manguel, who used to read to his fellow Argentine after he went blind, Borges would listen to passages from great writers and then show how they worked 'by taking paragraphs apart with the amorous intensity of a clockmaker'. Yet he felt able to lecture on the language of *Finnegans Wake* without having made great inroads into Joyce's novel, and he had little time for Proust, Tolstoy, Austen and Flaubert. He was often content to read plot summaries and the digests provided in encyclopaedias. As his French translator put it, 'He is all gaps.'

No matter how much we read, this is true of all of us. Like Borges, though, and like Proust, we can always fill those gaps with our favourite subject: ourselves.

THE QUIZ

N.B. The answers to most, but not all, of the questions are explicit in the text

1. Which character in *Hamlet* is Shakespeare supposed to have played?
2. How did William Tyndale die?
3. By what name do we usually know the broad-shouldered Aristocles?
4. Who married a woman whose name was an 'omen of felicitous adhesion'?
5. Whose erudition is 'a kind of damp which might in due time saturate a neighbouring body'?
6. What is intertextuality?
7. What does 'Islam' literally mean?
8. Who supposedly practised regulated hatred?
9. With which philosopher's razor would you not want to shave?
10. On whose stomach would you find the words 'Quod me nutrit me destruit', and in a portrait of which playwright do those words also appear?

11. Which poet kept a pet bear while at Cambridge, and suggested that it should sit for a fellowship of his college?

12. Who was Alfred Agostinelli?

13. Which actor, originally from Montreal, links Shakespeare and Dostoevsky?

14. What was the working title of Margaret Mitchell's novel *Gone with the Wind*?

15. Who finds a nose in his fresh loaf of bread?

16. Which novel ends with the words 'yes I said yes I will Yes'?

17. What is the first line of Spenser's *The Faerie Queene*?

18. Which of the marriages in Jane Austen's novels involves the biggest age gap?

19. Where do Chaucer's May and Damyan have sex?

20. Which English monarch wrote a pamphlet about the dangers of consuming tobacco?

21. Who supposedly kept a stuffed parrot on his desk while writing a story about a servant girl called Félicité?

22. In which country was the novelist Roberto Bolaño born?

23. Whose 'bookish rule' was alleged to have harmed the fortunes of England?

24. What is the connection between *A Vindication of the Rights of Woman* and *Frankenstein*?

25. The film *10 Things I Hate About You* is based on which Shakespeare play?

26. According to Ezra Pound, what could only be justified if it proved a cure for venereal disease?

27. In Michael Almereyda's film of *Hamlet*, where does the hero deliver his most famous soliloquy?

28. Who is Cher Horowitz?

29. Which character speaks the largest percentage of the lines in Shakespeare's *Othello*?

30. Besides beef and beer, what are the so-called British beatitudes?

31. What is *haecceitas*?

32. Who was assisted by twenty-nine scribes?

33. Which novel has the epigraph 'Vengeance is mine; I will repay'?

34. Whose death is signalled by a blank chapter?

35. Which of Shakespeare's characters describes his lips as 'two blushing pilgrims'?

36. Who is generally considered to have been the first convert to Islam?

37. Who kept casual notes in volumes he called 'waste books'?

38. Who was C. K. Scott-Moncrieff?

39. Which seventeenth-century poet was the Member of Parliament for Hull?

40. 'Pyramid Song', which contains several allusions to Dante, is the work of which British band?

41. In which year was the Booker Prize first awarded?

42. What kills Daisy Miller?

43. Who impresses women on a train by talking about Bertolt Brecht?

44. Which political philosopher lived at 122 Regent's Park Road in Primrose Hill?

45. Whose style was described as 'curly' by his own brother?

46. Whose trousers were apparently so tight that you could count the small change in his pocket?

47. Which organization's motto is *In varietate concordia*?

48. In James Joyce's *Ulysses*, what goes *Pflaap*?
49. Whom did Dante's Beatrice marry?
50. What is Sturgeon's Law?

ACKNOWLEDGEMENTS

Here's a secret – it is often in a book's acknowledgements that you can uncover the true story of its creation: who commissioned it, who furnished its sexy title, who ironed out its various wrinkles, whose unpublished research was generously made available and whose succour was vital. But most people do not even glance at the acknowledgements pages of the books they have gobbled up, struggled through or cast aside.

In Bruce Curtis's *The Politics of Population: State Formation, Statistics, and the Census of Canada, 1840-1875*, a book which sounds as though it ought to be bone dry, the acknowledgements page includes this: 'I'm not going to make a list . . . You'd be bored [if I did] or you'd stop reading after you found your name or didn't . . . so consider yourself thanked and your help gratefully appreciated, unless you're the critic who rejected the project and said I should start over, in which case start over yourself, I'm done.'

Despite the appeal of that sort of approach, I am going to make a list, but it is a short one and contains few clues. Make what you will, dear reader, of the names of the people who helped me in some way while I worked on the volume you are holding: Jonty Claypole, Ben Cowley, Gesche Ipsen, Peter

James, Kwasi Kwarteng, David Lebor and James Scudamore. I am grateful to the following at John Murray: Nikki Barrow, Lucy Dixon, Helen Hawksfield, Roland Philipps and James Spackman. Finally, I am especially indebted to my trusting and clear-sighted editor Eleanor Birne, my agent Peter Straus, Richard Arundel, Robert Macfarlane, my ever-supportive parents, and my patient girlfriend Angela.

Bruce Curtis also innovates by including what he calls a 'counterlist', comprising items such as a dead apple tree, bits of old medicine bottles and the bowl from a clay pipe. These items punctuated the landscape of the place where he wrote his book. My own counterlist is comparatively prosaic: a Chinese USB cup warmer too small to accommodate any cup I actually drink from, an old company stamp associated with Midland Employers' Mutual Assurance Ltd, and an uplighter that gets so hot after more than half an hour's use that I have on many evenings had to shed half of my clothes while sweating over these pages.

The author and publisher would like to thank the following for permission to reproduce copyright material: extract from 'Our Lady of Walsingham' in *Lord Weary's Castle*, copyright 1946 and renewed 1974 by Robert Lowell, reprinted by permission of Houghton Mifflin Harcourt Publishing Company; extract from 'The Waste Land' by T. S. Eliot, from *Collected Poems*, published by Faber & Faber Ltd; extract from 'The Trees' and 'A Study of Reading Habits' by Philip Larkin, from *Collected Poems*, published by Faber & Faber Ltd.